A Doll's House

Ibsen's Myth of Transformation

Twayne's Masterwork Studies

Robert Lecker, General Editor

A Doll's House

Ibsen's Myth of Transformation

Errol Durbach

Twayne Publishers • Boston
A Division of G. K. Hall & Co.

A Doll's House: Ibsen's Myth of Transformation
Errol Durbach

Twayne's Masterwork Studies No. 75

Published by Twayne Publishers
A division of G. K. Hall & Co.
70 Lincoln Street
Boston, Massachusetts 02111

Copyediting supervised by Barbara Sutton.
Book production by Gabrielle B. McDonald.
Typeset in 10/14 Sabon with Modern Bernhard as display type
by Compset, Inc., Beverly, Massachusetts.

First published 1991.
10 9 8 7 6 5 4 3 2 1 (hc)
10 9 8 7 6 5 4 3 2 1 (pb)

The paper used in this publication meets the minimum requirements
of American National Standard for Information Sciences—Permanence
of Paper for Printed Library Materials, ANSI Z39.48-1984. ∞™

Printed and bound in the United States of America.

Library of Congress Cataloging-in-Publication Data

Durbach, Errol, 1941–
    A Doll's House : Ibsen's myth of transformation / Errol Durbach.
      p.   cm.—(Twayne's masterwork studies ; no. 75)
    Includes bibliographical references and index.
    ISBN 0-8057-9403-4 (alk. paper).—ISBN 0-8057-8147-1 (pbk. :
alk. paper)
    1. Ibsen, Henrik, 1828–1900. Dukkehjem.   I. Title.   II. Series.
PT8861.D87   1991
    839.8'226—dc20   91-12131

For Ruth, Edna, Nadja, and Miriam

contents

note on the references and acknowledgments

Ibsen wrote *A Doll's House* in a form of Dano-Norwegian known as Riksmål, the standard literary language of the period when Norway still bore traces of its 400 years of political domination by Denmark. This stark and austerely lovely language has now been absorbed into more colloquial patterns of Norwegian usage, and it is Ibsen's fate to exist almost exclusively in translation, even in his own country. Each successive act of translation, from Riksmål to Nynorsk to English, moves the *word* itself further and further from its original context of tones and flavors, and, because part of my analysis depends on a close reading of the text, I have chosen to make frequent reference to the language in which Ibsen first conceived his play. I do this in hopes that somewhere along the way Ibsen may speak more directly across the gaps of time and language to a new generation of readers acquainted with some of the governing concepts in *A Doll's House*.

The Riksmål edition of *Et Dukkehjem* from which I quote is in *Henrik Ibsen: Samlede Værker*, vol. 6 (Kristiania & København: Gyldendalske Boghandel, 1914), the third edition of Ibsen's collected works. Many fine translations of *A Doll's House* are available, from Henrietta Frances Lord's Victorian *Nora* to Rolf Fjelde's modern American *A Doll House*. I have chosen the magisterial edition translated by James Walter McFarlane, *The Oxford Ibsen*, vol. 5 (London: Oxford University Press, 1961). This eight-volume edition, with its excellent introduction, draft versions of the drama, and critical appendices, is a standard reference work for English readers of Ibsen and is on the shelves of most major libraries. Page references in the text refer to these two editions of *Et Dukkehjem* and *A Doll's House* and appear in parentheses after the quoted passages. Other Ibsen plays quoted in English in the text also derive from *The Oxford Ibsen* and are cited in the text. Occasionally I offer my own translation of phrases or words when a more literal reading is necessary to make a point.

I am indebted to the many Ibsen scholars and editors who have contributed over the years to the critical discussions of *A Doll's House* and whose writing has been a constant challenge and guide to the understanding of Ibsen's play. There are few plays more open to disagreement, and I gratefully acknowledge in the Selected Bibliography the sources for a wide range of divergent arguments that have permeated my consciousness and my responses to Ibsen's play.

Excerpts from *A Doll's House* in *The Oxford Ibsen,* translated and edited by James Walter McFarlane, are reprinted by permission of Oxford University Press.

On a more personal note, I would like to thank Ruth, Edna, Nadja, and Miriam—mother, wife, daughter, and sister—who have enlarged my sense of the dolls' house and the way in which it operates and may be resisted in the modern world.

Henrik Ibsen
Portrait by Erik Werenskiold, 1895

chronology: henrik ibsen's life and works

1828	Henrik Ibsen born 20 March 1828 at Skien, in southeast Norway, to a prosperous merchant family.
1834	Father's bankruptcy mars Ibsen's childhood with poverty and social humiliation.
1844	At age 15 is sent to Grimstad, an isolated seaport farther down the coast, as assistant to an apothecary. Spends the next seven years ministering to the sick, stealing time from his duties to educate himself for university studies and write poetry.
1846	Fathers an illegitimate son by a servant 10 years his senior and pays paternity costs for the next 14 years.
1849	Writes first major drama, *Catiline*, a revisionist romantic verse play about a Roman rebel-hero.
1850	Prepared for university entrance examinations, leaves for Christiania (now Oslo). Defeated by Greek and mathematics, abandons plans for a medical career and writes *The Warrior's Barrow*, a play redolent with the spirit of national romanticism, which is staged in Christiania.
1851	Ole Bull recognizes a kindred soul in Ibsen and appoints him as general theatrical dogsbody to the newly formed National Theater in Bergen. Here he spends the next six years learning the business of theater—writing plays, keeping the books, stage-managing, blocking scenes, designing costumes, and mounting productions. In Bergen, learns the craft of dramaturgy by negative example and writes a series of saga plays that by contemporary standards are mostly unsuccessful.
1852	The only other advantage of his Bergen appointment is a subsidized study-tour to Copenhagen (where he sees Shakespeare performed for the first time) and Dresden (where he cultivates his interest in European art).

1857   Leaves Bergen to become the artistic director of the Norwegian Theater in Christiania.

1858–1861   Marries Suzannah Thoresen with whom he has a son. But his career in the theater moves steadily downhill. Public taste remains impervious to change, and his own work is consistently condemned. Impoverishment, debt, alcoholism, and apathy beset him.

1862   After a five-year period of writer's block, he finally produces *Love's Comedy*, a small masterpiece that his own theater rejects. He feels "excommunicated" and does little to arrest his theater's steady slide toward bankruptcy and closure.

1863–1864   Ill fortune turns and Ibsen is given a travel grant by the government (augmented by private donation), and this enables him to leave a country characterized, in his view, by small-mindedness, parochial taste, and reactionary politics. Publishes a scathing indictment of his countrymen in the poem "To Norway" and leaves home for 27 years.

1864   Discovers that prophets without honor in their own country soon acquire it in self-imposed exile; settles with his family in Rome.

1865–1866   Writes and publishes *Brand*, a verse allegory about an uncompromising idealist whose unyielding virtues wreak havoc in his life. It is widely acclaimed and wins him international recognition and an annual state pension from the Norwegian government.

1867   *Brand* is followed by its dialectical counterpart, *Peer Gynt,* a verse allegory about a fantasist whose lack of responsible commitment erodes his identity. The idealist and the fantasist will constitute the polarities of dramatic temperament in most of the plays that follow.

1868–1871   Ibsen moves to Dresden, where he edits, revises, and publishes his poetry before turning exclusively toward what he calls "the far more difficult art of prose."

1873   Completes a monumental two-part world historical epic, *Emperor and Galilean,* which contains a brilliant interplay of dialectical opposites in search of reconciliation in some third empire of the spirit. It establishes the framework of Ibsen's philosophical ideas, each linked thematically from play to play in the series of contemporary and more or less realistic dramas that follows.

1875   After a brief return visit to Norway, leaves to take up residence in Munich. This marks a watershed in his writing career—a turning away from saga plays, historical epic, and verse allegories toward a form of contemporary realism in a deliberately colloquial language.

1877   *The Pillars of Society* is the first of the realist plays and is a cause célèbre in Europe.

1879   *A Doll's House* is the second play in the series, written in 1879 (the year of the light bulb), while Ibsen lives in Rome and Amalfi. The play is published in Copenhagen, where it is also first staged—a genuinely European phenomenon.

1881   *Ghosts.*

1882   During his residence in Rome, writes *An Enemy of the People.*

1884   *The Wild Duck.*

1885–1890   After another brief visit to Norway, returns to Munich where he writes three great psychological studies of women: *Rosmersholm* (1886), *The Lady from the Sea* (1888), and *Hedda Gabler* (1890).

1889   At age 60 has a brief and mainly epistolary "affair" with 18-year-old Emilie Bardach.

1891   Returns to Norway, and the landscape of ice peaks, frozen snowfields, and permafrost not only surrounds the protagonists of his last plays but enters their souls.

1892   *The Master Builder.*

1894   *Little Eyolf.*

1896   *John Gabriel Borkman.*

1899   Last play, *When We Dead Awaken.*

1900   Suffers the first of a series of debilitating strokes that will eventually take his life.

1906   Dies 23 May at age 78.

LITERARY AND
HISTORICAL CONTEXT

1

The Spiritual Revolution

Nora slams the door of her doll's house in 1879, and the note of explosive defiance reverberates around the world. Nora's liberal impulse belongs not only to the history of women's liberation, but also to the problematic context of an age in which the free spirit must define itself in a world reshaped by a series of revolutions in social and political life. Ibsen's first play, *Catiline* (1849), as Brian Downs suggests in his book *Ibsen: The Intellectual Background,* is a dramatic response to the political revolution of 1848 and reveals the iconoclastic bias of Ibsen's thought: "In so far as radicalism and the cry for political liberty meant anything to him personally," writes Downs, "they always implied the emancipation of the individual from the restraint of magistrates and majorities."[1]

But even in the great bourgeois democracy, where the new middle-class Helmers settle into houses made comfortable by free enterprise capitalism, there are Noras who must free themselves from the *embourgeoisement* of spirit in a world dominated by the view of the silent majority. The revolutionary impulse has modulated between *Catiline* and *A Doll's House* from a cry for political revolution to a revolution that involves the human spirit first defining the limitations imposed on it by custom and then transforming itself—in defiance, if necessary, of that comfortable, hard-won bourgeois democracy.

The very idea of self-transformation and redefinition is implicit in the cultural history of Norway in the nineteenth century. Freed from four centuries of Danish rule in 1814, modern Norway emerged as the fulfillment of the political dream of the age of revolution—a sovereign nation, born in the spirit of bloodless revolution with a democratic constitution and in search of national identity and a national language. Ibsen was born into the heady cultural climate of Norwegian nationhood, but as he grew up he developed a sense of disillusionment with the course that national identity was assuming—an unreal and sentimental romanticism on the one hand and a reversion to reactionary politics on the other. In 1864, when Prussia declared war on Denmark, Norway, instead of striking a blow for independence and freedom, did nothing. Ibsen, appalled at this apathetic failure to assert Scandinavian solidarity with decisive action, recognized in his countrymen the Troll who tempts Peer Gynt to a kind of complacent self-sufficiency that is synonymous with self-defeat. *Peer Gynt* is the archetypal Norwegian antihero of selfhood. Nora Helmer is his antithesis.

Fifty years of cultural history—a mood of steadily increasing prosperity and optimism in the long peaceful European summer, strikingly countermanded by a sense of spiritual entropy and encroaching loss—are finally brought to a crisis in *A Doll's House.* The liberating impulses of the age of revolution have gradually succumbed to the temptations of materialism, and the romantic spirit either accommodates itself unwittingly to the sufficiencies of a middle-class Eden (like Nora in the first two acts) or (like Hedda Gabler in Ibsen's later play) turns its weapons furiously against the restraints of reality that curtail all aspirations toward the sublime. In *A Doll's House,* the romantic energies of David's Napoleon crossing the Alps—a mighty, windswept image of infinite potential—have been reduced, as it were, to a cheap reproduction hung over the mantelpiece as a memory of forfeited greatness. Nora's residual "Romanticism" has been trivialized in the bourgeois parlor to a type of small "r" sentimentality, and Ibsen issues the challenge of bringing into creative alliance the recovered energies of spirit with the new realities of the postrevolutionary, postromantic world.

To regain authenticity for Nora, Ibsen must find an authentic language in which to speak of the revolution in the soul, a new vocabulary sculpted out of the old lexicon, just as the newborn Norway needed to dredge a national idiom out of Danish syntax. There is the sense throughout Ibsen's drama of the search in a pre-Freudian age to discover a notation of the inner life, some way of speaking about what the Norwegian novelist Hamsun in the 1890s would call "*det ubevidste sjæleliv*"; "the unconscious life of the mind." Ibsen must now make crucial distinctions between pleasure and joy, between mere satisfaction and an indispensable condition of living, between the materially wonderful and the spiritually miraculous. Ibsen's language in *A Doll's House* is beginning to chart the progress of "*sjæleliv*"—mind, soul, psyche, spirit—into a new dimension of human cultural identity where the romantic definition of mankind blends with the existential in an essentially modern amalgam. Words begin to modulate, for example, *vidunderlig* or "marvelous," filtered through the reorganizing consciousness until the new idea of a "miracle" is hammered out of old material, and, from play to play, Ibsen's neologisms—like *lysrædd* or "light fear," *livslogen* or "life lie"—begin to shape a changing phenomenology of human existence.

PHILOSOPHICAL INFLUENCES

Brian Johnston's thesis, consistently argued in a number of publications, is that Ibsen's place in the intellectual life of the nineteenth century is beside Hegel and that Ibsen's last 12 plays recapitulate the German philosopher's history of human consciousness in *The Phenomenology of Mind* (1807).[2] Because Ibsen was notoriously shifty about sources and influences, it is difficult to establish incontrovertible links between his thinking and the great contemporary minds of the nineteenth century. But whether he absorbed their ideas through a process of cultural osmosis from the zeitgeist, or more directly from his reading or his limited tenure as a student in Christiania, it remains quite clear that the *form* shaping his thought was Hegel's dialectical method: one stage of human consciousness colliding with another in a process of continuous historical transformation. My only reservation about applying a thoroughgoing Hegelian model to Ibsen's drama is its failure to admit a fallible human identity to these incarnated intellectual absolutes. Ibsen's people live as vitally in the guts as they do in the *geist* (spirit), and despite their close affinity with Hegel's stages of evolving consciousness, his characters are enveloped in irony and paradox that frequently deny the absolutes of Hegel's ideal vision—just as Ibsen's dramatic structure habitually resists synthesis of opposites in conflict.

Michael Meyer, Ibsen's biographer, relates a deathbed incident that sums up both the life and the work.[3] To the group of concerned family and friends surrounding the bed of the comatose Ibsen, the nurse attending him offers some cheery reassurance—he seems to be a little better. Ibsen regains sufficient consciousness to contradict her. *"Tvertimod!"* he retorts—"On the contrary." These are his last words and are perfectly consistent with an essentially dialectical frame of mind: an ability to entertain an idea and its opposite in a single visionary moment and a willingness to acknowledge that truth exists as a shifting point between two contradictory extremes.

If Ibsen borrowed from his contemporaries, he always did so with a keen sense of the contradiction—the *tvertimod*—at the heart of human experience, and his radical skepticism ensured that all philosophies were tested *"i hjertets og hjernens hvælv"*; "in the depths of the heart and the brain."[4]

Ibsen has also been called Kierkegaard's poet, but his discipleship to the great Danish existentialist is qualified by his questioning of the conclusions that Kierkegaard draws from shared philosophical premises. Like Kierkegaard, Ibsen recognizes selfhood as the sum total of necessary human choices—even in the face of dreadful anxiety and uncertainty. For Kierkegaard, the self is redeemed by defining itself in the will of God. But for Ibsen's heroines, like Nora and Hedda Gabler and Rebekka (*Rosmersholm*), choosing selfhood becomes irremediably tragic when God's presence is no longer discernible and mankind must exercise divine prerogative in a world devoid of certainties. In this sense, critic Eric Bøgh's cruel image of Nora as a "Kierkegaard in skirts"[5] is at least a half-truth in that, to the faithful, she would seem to endorse the Kierkegaardian leap into the absurd where the hand of God is waiting to cradle the newly created essence. But in *A Doll's House,* as in Ibsen's drama generally, the "miraculous" is never synonymous with divine intervention or the discovery of selfhood as some essential abstraction. Selfhood must first choose its existence, even at the risk of cancelling the vital roles that shape the old self—as Nora must cancel the relationships that sustain her as mother and wife—and the new self must assume responsibility for shaping the consequences of a choice that secures her freedom at terrible cost.

•   •   •

Whatever his differences from the great formative thinkers who preceded him, Ibsen's vision coincided with theirs on at least one crucial point: a belief in man's extraordinary capacity to free himself from static and determined systems, to participate in his own self-transformation and to impel a revolution from within. The worldview of the 1870s was shaped as much by Darwin and the new Naturalistic sciences as by the philosopher-prophets of the century. The scientific vision of humankind, endorsed by theorists like Zola, by sociologists like Comte, by Bernard's treatise on *Experimental Medicine* (1865), and by Hippolyte Taine's *History of English Literature* (1864), stressed the species' awful entrapment by the united forces of heredity, environment, and history, the humiliation of romantic aspiration by the lump of physiological raw material in which it is encased, and a universe wherein only physical strength and the jungle law prevail. This frame of mind dominates the world of *A Doll's House,* with its recurrent discussions of genetic inheritance, congenital disease, the transmission of moral corruption, the power of parental influence, and the ever-present pressure of the dolls' house itself.

Ibsen depicts a middle-class milieu in which a type of small-mindedness is disastrously coupled with those attitudes that envision the world as a macaroon-filled paradise snugly insulated against the horrors of external reality. Nora's triumph is freeing herself from generations of social and intellectual conditioning, from the twin gods of scientific determinism, heredity and environment, and from the encarcerating thought processes that strip her of self-worth, self-determination, and authentic selfhood. In stepping out of her doll's house, Nora also steps out of the historical context of the late nineteenth century into a challenging modernity, with its stringent demands upon those defenseless individuals who dare to strike out for freedom.

2

The Importance of the Work

For theater historians from Shaw to Steiner, the importance of *A Doll's House* derives mainly from its "technical novelty" and from Ibsen's discovery of a significant modern theater of effective myth and symbolic action. In his realistic drama, writes George Steiner in *The Death of Tragedy* (1961), Ibsen finally triumphed where every major playwright after Shakespeare had failed: "he created a new mythology and the theatrical conventions with which to express it."[1] By the early 1970s, however, Ibsen's revolutionary stagecraft was no longer seen as the foremost achievement of his genius in *A Doll's House*. In her book *Sexual Politics* (1970), Kate Millett sees Ibsen as the first dramatist since the Greeks to challenge the myth of male dominance: "In Aeschylus' dramatization of the myth, one is permitted to see patriarchy confront matriarchy, confound it through the knowledge of paternity, and come off triumphant. Until Ibsen's Nora slammed the door announcing the sexual revolution, this triumph went nearly uncontested."[2] In the 1980s another generation of readers and scholars has uncovered other themes in the play—from a Hegelian allegory where pagan values collide with Christian[3] to a rejection of the resurgent narcissism of the "me" generation.[4]

Perspectives on the enduring classics keep changing, and the dynamism of *A Doll's House*—its ability to keep sustaining new readings—compels us to return to the text, to stage the play again and again so that new shards of truth may come to light in the varieties of performance. *A Doll's House* finally liberates us from preconception, sets us painfully free from a secure but potentially self-demeaning middle-class value system, and confronts us with the necessary difficulty of choosing an authentic identity and giving it substance. It reveals the close affinity of liberation and tragedy, of exhilaration and catastrophe, and, perhaps most importantly, it insists on the *normative* quality of experience, its universal accessibility. The grandeur of Ibsen's vision does not derive from the social elevation of heroism, but from its ordinariness. Nora's achievement lies within our own capacity should we make that choice, and if we are unable to emulate Hamlet or Lear, we can at least admire the lady next door who slams the door on a lifetime of comfortable self-deception.

"Ibsen gave us a new worldview," wrote the dramatist Wedekind, "a new picture of man,"[5] and Ibsen achieved this through the technical novelty of the realistic stage, by generating an image of selfhood redefined in the modern world and by incarnating the revolutionary protagonist as a housewife in a bourgeois parlor. *A Doll's House* is not a sudden incursion of existentialism into Ibsen's concerns. Its foundations are laid in the great verse allegories of the 1860s, and especially in Ibsen's deeply ironic speculation on the nature of the self in *Peer Gynt* (1867), where all the inherited philosophies of selfhood are scrutinized and reexamined. Classical selfhood demands that we *know* ourselves, but in the modern world, knowing oneself is insufficient as a life purpose. The important path, as Kierkegaard's philosophy makes clear, is to *choose* our selves and construct identity out of decision, action, and commitment—to *make* something of our lives. This injunction is a radical challenge, as well, to romanticism, which defines the self as unlimited potential, the abstract idea of all our imperishable dreams and hopes. For Ibsen, the fallibility of the romantic vision lies in its failure to account for mankind's regressive tendencies, his Troll-like affinity with the beast beneath the skin and the complacent sort of self-satisfaction that ends by annihilating selfhood. For the Troll never commits himself, never chooses, and his self atrophies and dwindles into a form of comfortable nonbeing. The other side of romantic self-definition is the imaginative fiction, the Bovaryism, that submerges the self in fantasy and finally insulates it against all contact with reality. Authentic selfhood, as Peer Gynt never quite grasps, is not an invisible, unrealized potential, however lovely the dream. Instead it comes into being by confronting reality and by choosing the difficulty and the suffering that this demands.

If *Peer Gynt* marks the end point of the romantic worldview that defines self as "soul" and permits abstractions in place of actions, then *A Doll's House* posits the existential counterproposition: the notion that the individual defines the self by transforming potential into actuality, wish-dreams into facts, and ideals into realities. Nora discovers, in her intense experience, the Sartrean life formula that "existence precedes essence"—that the willed decision and the action must anticipate the merely abstract idea of her personal significance and give it substance. She is the living answer to Peer Gynt's ultimate question to the old buttonmolder: "What, after all, is this 'being one's self'?" And she embodies the buttonmolder's enigmatic reply in her creative/destructive choice to die as a doll in order to live the life of a woman:

BUTTONMOULDER:	To be one's self is to kill one's self.
	I doubt if that answer means anything to you.
	So we'll put it this way: to show unmistakably
	The Master's intention whatever you're doing.
PEER:	But what if a man has never discovered
	What the Master intended?
BUTTONMOULDER:	Then he must sense it. (*Peer Gynt,* 3:411)

Whether one reads *A Doll's House* as a technical revolution in modern theater, the modern tragedy, the first feminist play since the Greeks, a Hegelian allegory of the spirit's historical evolution, or a Kierkegaardian leap from aesthetic into ethical life, the deep structure of the play as a modern myth of self-transformation ensures it perennial importance as a work that honors the vitality of the human spirit in women *and* men. Nora finally shows us that "being one's self" is a process of continuous change, a transcendence of inauthentic dreams of selfhood and a "killing" of the old self as evidence of the Master's intention. And even if there is no Master, the Ibsen hero must have sufficient confidence in the self to think with the mind of God and embody this intention in enacted choice. Existence precedes essence, but without a sense of higher purpose, existence itself is paltry. If Nora's accomplishment is indeed "miraculous," the miracles of *A Doll's House* belong to a new and extraordinary form of secular faith.

3

Critical Reception

1879–1880: RESPONSES TO *A DOLL'S HOUSE* IN SCANDINAVIA AND GERMANY

Henrietta Frances Lord, the first reputable English translator of *A Doll's House*, was living in Stockholm when the play first appeared, and she has written about the intellectual excitement of the event, the buzz in cultivated homes where Ibsen was regarded as Scandinavia's great teacher. The play was published on 4 December 1879, a good two weeks before its first performance, and within a month the entire edition of 8,000 copies had been sold out and reprinted by Ibsen's Danish publisher. People were avidly reading *A Doll's House* as a significant *publishing* event, so even before the curtain rose in Copenhagen's Royal Theatre on 21 December the play was already a cause célèbre in Scandinavia. "Such furious discussion did *Nora* rouse when the play came out," writes Frances Lord, ". . . that many a social invitation given in Stockholm during that winter bore the words, 'You are requested not to mention Ibsen's *Doll's House*!' "[1]

Heated debate, difference of opinion in domestic parlors, and endless talk were the dominant responses to Ibsen's play after its opening in the major Scandinavian capitals in the New Year, in Stockholm, Christiania, Bergen, and Helsinki. The same is true of its contemporary reception in Germany. To add even more vehemence to the intense commotion, Ibsen was obliged by the management of the first German production to provide an alternative ending to the play. Hedwig Niemann-Raabe, a famous leading lady, had refused to perform on-stage an action that she would have found abhorrent in life: "*I* would never leave *my* children!" she declared. To forestall an even greater disaster to his text, Ibsen drafted a conciliatory ending in which Nora sinks to her knees at the doorway of the children's bedroom and abandons her emancipation for their good. (He called it a "barbaric outrage" to be used only in emergencies.) This was the version first seen in Flensburg in February 1880 and later in Hamburg, Dresden, Hanover, and Berlin. Ibsen attended the first authentic production at Munich's Residenztheater in March 1880 and reported on the response: "Down here *A Doll's House* has caused the same commotion as at home. People have come out passionately either for or against the play, and it has scarcely ever happened in Munich before that a drama has been so vehemently discussed as this."[2] When the original ending was eventually restored in Berlin, there were further altercations about the omission of a necessary fourth act ("Commentary," 457).

These responses are typical of the general public reaction to the play in Scandinavia and Europe. In 1879–80 *A Doll's House* did not precipitate heated debate about feminism, women's rights, or male domination. The sound and the fury were addressed to the very question that Hedwig Niemann-Raabe had so peremptorily settled: What wife and mother would ever walk out in this way on her family? What credible motivation could one adduce for such extraordinary behavior? And is it remotely feasible that the child-wife of act 1 could take the decisive action of the new woman of act 3? M. W. Brun's review of the play in *Folkets Avis* (24 December 1879) reveals the typical tone, audience concerns, and critical point of view of the period.[3] Ibsen, he declared, devastates the domestic pleasures so realistically dramatized in the first two acts and disgusts his audience by violating the conventional. He departs from "ordinary humanity" in order to "exalt the untrue" and in the process betrays the aesthetic, psychological, and dramatic values of the piece. "I ask you directly," Brun continues, buttonholing his readers, "is there one mother among thousands of mothers, one wife among thousands of wives, who would behave as Nora behaves, who would desert children, husband, and home merely in order to become 'a human being'? I answer with conviction: no and again no!" (Brun, 86). The drawing rooms of Scandinavia no doubt resounded with rhetoric as vehement as this. Habituated to decades of well-made social problem plays, the critics continue to isolate a "problem" in the dramatic text and then resolve it by dogmatic declaration. And if the problem will not simply go away, they berate Ibsen for leaving the issues annoyingly open to dissension and debate thereby violating the rules of dramatic structure in the search for novelty.

The critics clearly identified with Helmer, played with subtlety and brilliance by Emil Poulsen, who ensured a fine balance in the production: he played a chauvinist perhaps, but one whose depth of feeling and emotional conviction ensnared the sympathy of Brun and reinforced his bias against Nora's unnatural behavior. The drama critic of *Dags-Telegrafen,* similarly captivated by the specious Helmer, declared Helmer's greatest offense his choice of a frivolous girl as his wife. The reviews merely reinforced Ibsen's general observation in his notes for *A Doll's House* that women in contemporary society have no autonomous selfhood independent of men's image of them: "it is an exclusively male society with laws drafted by men, and with counsel and judges who judge feminine conduct from the male point of view" (436). Edvard Brandes[4] was one of the few contemporary critics of the play to caution his readers against the myopia of Helmer's perspective, which merely subsumes, without investigation, the mindless and reactionary views of his society. It is at least likely that in the commotion stirred up by the *Doll's House* debate in the bourgeois parlors of Europe a few wives and mothers would have cut Helmer down to size even if—like Hedwig Niemann-Raabe—their choice might have been to stay at home and mind the children.

In 1879 *A Doll's House* was decidedly *not* a myth of spiritual transformation but a problem play: a social problem, a moral problem, and, above all, a psychological problem that challenged credibility. Nora's transformation was pronounced an impossibility, a ridiculous and ill-prepared transition from "a little Nordic Frou-Frou" (as Erich Bøgh described her) into a "Søren Kierkegaard in skirts."[5] Her momentous change, so carefully anticipated in the text, was measured against the subjective criteria of psychological realism and dismissed as clumsy dramaturgy. It is extraordinary to encounter such obdurate denials of Nora's capacity to change, such determination on the part of Ibsen's readers to ignore her steady clarification of consciousness from crisis to crisis in the dramatic action and the growth of moral intelligence that drives the play toward its dénouement. Critics predisposed, like Helmer, to believe in the ineluctable and inevitable forces of heredity and social conditioning were apparently incapable of acknowledging the existential implications of the play— its insistence on humankind's capacity to recast the contents of the mind and transform the nature of the soul. Too distracted by contemporary "problems," too limited by their own worldview, they merely denied what is basic to Ibsen's dramatic vision.

Moreover, as Frederick and Lise-Lone Marker suggest in their study "The First Nora," Betty Hennings's interpretation of the role, however well received, might have set a precedent for the improbable switch from "Nordic Frou-Frou" to a "Kierkegaard in skirts." Hennings failed to rise to the challenge of discovering the mature and self-respecting woman in the frivolous macaroon-nibbling child-wife of act 1. Instead, she played a fractured personality, devoid of those moments of continuous self-revelation that constitute the major objective of the role and fashion psychological complexity out of a steady accumulation of morally shocking surprises. Without the divided consciousness that can register and learn from its own failures of insight and perception, the actress playing Nora runs the risk of performing two inadequately integrated roles and creating yet another distracting "problem" for the critics to debate.

The critical reception of the play in Scandinavia leaves one with the impression of public and critical dissent about the credibility of Nora's defection from the dolls' house and almost complete indifference to the spiritual implications of her revolutionary choice.

1880–1889: RESPONSES TO
A DOLL'S HOUSE IN ENGLAND

In England the translation of *A Doll's House* preceded the first significant stage production there by at least six years. In the history of both the publication and the performance, however, there were a number of false (if not positively ridiculous) starts. T. Weber, a Danish schoolmaster, produced an English translation in 1880 that survives only as a model of gobbledegook and is comparable in silliness to the first dramatic adaptation of *A Doll's House*, entitled *Breaking a Butterfly* (1884), by Henry Arthur Jones and Henry Herman. In making Ibsen's play into a well-made melodrama wherein the more unrealistic of Nora's wish-dreams (and those of the English theater-going public) are happily satisfied, Jones and Herman merely reversed the Ibsen revolution and restored the play to the very tradition it had subverted five years before.

Even among responsible critics and translators there was a certain resistance to Ibsen's vision in the play. Henrietta Frances Lord produced a fairly straightforward translation, entitled *Nora*, in 1882, but she prefaced it with an eccentric essay on karma and heredity and the doctrine of twin souls. This was the version used for one of the first public readings in England of an Ibsen play, and the context of this reading speaks volumes for his peculiar critical reception among the English intelligentsia. In January 1886, Karl Marx's youngest daughter, Eleanor, feeling that she "*must* do something to make people understand our Ibsen a little more than they do,"[6] invited a select gathering to the house she shared with her common-law husband, Edward Aveling, in Great Russell Street. Bernard Shaw was among her invited guests—it was his first time he had seen a performance of an

Ibsen play—and he played Krogstad to the Mrs. Linde of William Morris's daughter, May.

For the English Ibsenites, the Norwegian Master was full of ideological fervor, a champion of political causes from Marxism and Fabianism to secularism, hedonism, and atheism. Eleanor Marx played Nora to Aveling's Torvald, roles that they acted with the utter conviction that the "miracle" had already taken place in their pleasant house in Great Russell Street. The couple had just published an article called "The Woman Question: From a Socialist Point of View" in which they argued that when the revolution came—and Eleanor believed that *A Doll's House* was its harbinger—men and women would be joined in free contract, mind to mind, as a whole and completed entity. For Marxists, *A Doll's House* envisioned the emancipation of men and women from the capitalist system with the abolition of class rule serving as a prerequisite for the abolition of sex rule, and because, for Eleanor Marx, the status of women in society was directly analogous to that of the proletariat, she submerged all interest in sectarian feminism into the larger issues of social change through revolutionary action. For her, Nora's predicament was a metaphor for the oppression and exploitation of the working classes, and marriage in Ibsen's play symbolized the last bastion of serfdom recognized by law. The resounding door slam was viewed as the first rumble of momentous social rebellion, and if Ibsen's play ends on a note of tenuous possibility that some secular "miracle" might transform Christmas into a celebration of cultural renewal, for Eleanor Marx that "miracle" was socialism, which would bring economic and intellectual emancipation for women and workers alike. "Even Ibsen has failed us"[7] was the unhappy conclusion she would later reach, having turned "Ibsenism" into a banner for her own political purposes. The appalling failure of her "marriage" with Edward Aveling and the disintegration of her fervent political ideals, no doubt, contributed to her suicide.

Eleanor Marx's reading of *A Doll's House* is an extreme instance of the Ibsenism generated by the play: it became entangled in various causes that were partly political, partly personal. But, as Ian Britain has argued,[8] if we examine Shaw's response to Ibsen and the responses of other political thinkers, it soon becomes apparent that they were as interested in his dramatic poetry as in his ideas. Shaw's lecture to the Fabian Society in 1890 flatly denies that Ibsen's thesis is socialist. Ibsen's plays, said Shaw, are a dire warning to people who "deliberately let themselves be idealized into doing what they don't like."[9] He defined "Ibsenism" as a rejection, in politics as in other spheres of life, of the distractions of idealism in favor of practical reality.

When the Fabian lecture was expanded into *The Quintessence of Ibsenism* (1891, 1912–13), its dominating emphasis was aesthetic rather than political. For Shaw, the Ibsen revolution was not another form of socialism but a *theatrical* rout in which the Norwegian Master battled the worldview and the value systems of spiritually moribund well-made plays with new forms and a new poetics of modern drama. Shaw was captivated by the *technical* and not the *political* novelty of the new drama, and together with a staunch band of literary colleagues—most notably Edmund Gosse and Ibsen's first systematic translator and critic, William Archer—he guided audience responses to the play, described their reactions, and poured scorn on the censorious abuse that was showered upon the first professional performance of *A Doll's House* in England.

This first performance took place on 7 June 1889 and was produced by Charles Charrington, with Janet Achurch, his wife, playing Nora. The quintessential Ibsenites were there to hail it: critic Harley Granville-Barker declared it "the most dramatic event of the decade;"[10] William Archer published an essay on the play in the *Fortnightly Review* on 1 July declaring Ibsen the most famous man in the English literary world.[11] Shaw published his unsigned review in the *Manchester Guardian* on 8 June, praising the play's power to compel the audience's acquiescence in an action that they did not quite comprehend.[12] Like dragons at the gate of public censure, Ibsen's great defenders were in place to breathe wrath upon small-minded criticism—Archer's dismissal of Clement Scott and Shaw's of Robert Buchanan, for example, confidently assert the context in which Ibsen should be understood in England.[13] These contexts, over time, may appear rather quaint and quixotic, but they constitute the mainstream of English dramatic criticism in the 1890s and render irrelevant the squeals of journalistic outrage that heralded Ibsen's arrival in England. Archer's most cunning rebuttal to the anti-Ibsenite reviewers was simply publishing their remarks without comment, confident that the English public would share his scorn. Here is a sampling of the material he recorded in 1893: "It would be a misfortune were such a morbid and unwholesome play to gain the favour of the public" (*Standard*); "Unnatural, immoral, and in its concluding scene, essentially undramatic" (*People*); "Strained deductions, lack of wholesome human nature, pretentious inconclusiveness. . . . Cannot be allowed to pass without a word of protest against the dreary and sterilizing principle which it seeks to embody" (*Observer*).[14] By the time Archer came to reprint these comments, however, the *Standard* no longer represented the usual view of Ibsen, the *People* merely misrepresented public opinion, and the *Observer* seemed devoid of intelligent observation. Ibsen had become the dramatist of the avant-garde, the spokesman of liberal values in Europe, and the author of the kind of publications on Mrs. Alving's table that so shock Pastor Manders in *Ghosts*, a reputation he retained for decades. In Sean O'Casey's *Juno and the Paycock* (1924) the shiftless and drunken Captain Boyle stumbles upon a volume of Ibsen's plays (including *A Doll's House*) among his daughter's things. "Nothin' but thrash," he assures his drinking buddy, ". . . buks only fit for chiselurs!"[15] But the derisive comment has itself become the object of derision, and the Ibsen volume on O'Casey's stage set now signals the audience that a complex of progressive and liberating ideas threatens Captain Boyle's doll's house republic of chauvinistic self-delusion and flight from reality.

1882–1906: RESPONSES TO *A DOLL'S HOUSE* IN AMERICA

When Ibsen's heroine, Lona Hessel, returns from America to the cramped Norway of *Pillars of Society,* she brings with her the liberating spirit of the New World, which Ibsen envisions as the domain of light and freedom and truth. But America did not reciprocate the compliment. "We are glad to announce that Haverly's Minstrels will relieve the Ibsen gloom next Monday night,"[16] wrote one critic of the touring production of *Ghosts* in 1906. Although the *Morning Appeal* of Carson City, Nevada, may not represent the highest caliber of dramatic comment, it surely indicates that Haverly's Minstrels rather than *Ghosts* was the standard definition of theater in America before the advent of Provincetown and the drama of O'Neill. In Germany, France, and England there were theaters to receive Ibsen and dramatists open to his influence, but in America, as the editor of *Independent* pointed out in writing Ibsen's obituary notice, "Ibsen has exerted no such influence, because there are no such dramatists to be influenced. . . . An American Ibsen would starve."[17] Ibsen's gloom belonged to the pessimistic European past, to the Old World that Americans had put behind them. His philosophy, as Robert Schanke puts it, was "un-American", and "since the plays written by the Norwegian poet of gloom reflected European culture, they were considered misanthropic, anarchistic, and unsuited for healthy Americans."[18] "There is nothing for Americans in Ibsen," Edward Dithmar warned Minnie Fiske,[19] one of the early American Noras (1894), and echoing the dire prediction, made after the first professional production of the play in Louisville, Kentucky, that Ibsen would "never become very popular with American audiences" (Schanke, vii). (In the worst traditions of the American commercial theater, a dismissive review had ended the run of Modjeska's *Thora* after a single performance in 1883.) And this is the critical climate in which Ibsen and *A Doll's House* made their inauspicious American debut.

The first transatlantic Nora was the eponymous *Child Wife* of 1882, an adaptation of Ibsen's play by William Moore Lawrence, staged in Milwaukee, Wisconsin, and starring Minerva Guernsey in the title role. It included an Irish widow for laughs, a child's song for sentiment, and a happy ending for audience satisfaction. (A similarly upbeat ending would fail to save Modjeska's unlucky *Thora* in the following year.) Not until 1889 was an authentic *Doll's House*, in

Archer's translation, seen in America. This Richard Mansfield production, with Beatrice Cameron as Nora, toured extensively and attracted the sort of anti-Ibsen notices that would have delighted Archer with their hospital-ward rhetoric. Morally disgusted critics inveighed against the "horrible oozings" of festering sores smeared repulsively over everything, the vision of jaundiced eyes, and so on and so forth. In Philadelphia, Schanke recounts, ill-informed parents lined up with their offspring to see what they mistakenly believed was a new play for children (Schanke, 11).

By 1895, however, it was unlikely that the public would remain ignorant of the contents of *A Doll's House*. There were three productions that year, with Mrs. Fiske repeating her 1894 performance in a benefit for the maternity and training school departments of Hannemann Hospital (an extraordinarily unnerving play for expectant mothers, one would think). Mrs. Fiske, however, rendered *A Doll's House* suitably aseptic by expurgating all its sexuality, together with the silk stockings, the emotional passion of the tarantella, and Dr. Rank's references to his disease. Her performance stressed the child-wife, again, complete with baby talk and silly self-esteem. But she failed to find the resolute woman within the comedienne, and although she repeated the role again in 1902, it continued to elude her. She finally dropped Nora from her repertoire, although she had established it as the test role for subsequent generations of American actresses.

One of the few to rise nobly to the challenge of playing Nora was Ethel Barrymore, who in 1905 restored to the part all the passion and intensity that Minnie Fisk had so decorously concealed. By this time, moreover, there was an informed audience of emancipated American women to register the extent of Nora's suffering in the doll's house and to question the assumptions propping up its structure. If Mrs. Fiske had been acting in a vacuum, Ethel Barrymore was now acting in a context and challenging the misguided notion that there was nothing for Americans in Ibsen (Schanke, 22–23).

It was not until after his death in 1906, however, that the dramatist gained a sort of American dramatic "citizenship," with the American intelligentsia leaping Archer-like to his reevaluation and defense. Edwin Slosson, in his editorial obituary "Ibsen as an Interpreter of American Life," read into Ibsen's Norwegian provincials the same individuality that he discerned in provincial America and the same revolutionary impulse toward the "victories of self-assertion over the oppression of society, and of naked truth over conventional shams" (Egan, 454). His Ibsen is the disillusioned democrat, the guardian against the tyrannies of tradition, conventionality, and public opinion, a "layer of ghosts and pricker of bubbles" for whom Americans stand in need (Egan, 454). This reappraisal is echoed in William Dean Howells's obituary[20] in the *North American Review* (July 1906), where he argues that Ibsen forces us to question our best intentions, the springs of action, and the very grounds of our conviction. And, like the best of Ibsen's English critics, Howells also sees him as a poet of the theater, "a poet of such absolute simplicity and veracity, that when I read him or see him I feel nothing wanting in the aesthetic sense" (Egan, 446).

James Gibbons Huneker added his powerful critical voice to these speeches of acceptance by other American shapers of opinion, and Ibsen, after years of repudiation as "un-American" in thought and feeling, was finally admitted, posthumously, to the spiritual homeland he had extolled in *The Pillars of Society* some 30 years before.

A READING

4

Translating Et Dukkehjem *into* A Doll's House

Et Dukkehjem, Ibsen's original Dano-Norwegian title, slips quite easily into its English equivalent *A Doll's House* because an image of cozy middle-class married life had already been well established in the Victorian novel 15 years before Ibsen's play: "Well! And so we live on Blackheath, in the charm—ingest of dolls' houses, de—lightfully furnished, and we have a clever little servant, who is de—cidedly pretty, and we are economical and orderly, and do everything by clockwork, and we have a hundred and fifty pounds a year, and we have all we want and more."[1] There is a repellent cuteness to the quality of life described by the heroine of Dickens's *Our Mutual Friend* (1864–65), a cloying tone of smug self-satisfaction that envelops her Blackheath paradise, and Dickens's careful placement of his apostrophe in "dolls' house" incorporates all the inhabitants of this little world and reduces them to a common level of mechanized domestic bliss. They are all dolls—as most certainly are the characters in Ibsen's play, and there is a good case for altering the standard English translation of Ibsen's title to clarify this metaphor.[2] But neither "a dolls' house" nor "a doll house" quite captures the tonalities and connotations of Ibsen's "*dukkehjem*"—a dolls' *home,* a snug haven, a world of private domestic ideals presided over by a paragon of wifely duty, populated by perfect doll children, and protected by a model paterfamilias. A "house" is not necessarily a "home." I shall retain the customary title *A Doll's House* when referring to the play and "the dolls' house" when dealing with the sociological phenomenon that is the play's subject—the world of middle-class values and assumptions.

Translation is not merely a matter of shifting some words from one language into another. It demands a shift in cultural attitudes, an imaginative bridging of gaps between the last century and this one. If we pride ourselves that we no longer live in dolls' houses, it is because plays like Ibsen's have undermined so thoroughly the Victorian foundations of "home" and "family," exposing them as empty and oppressive shams in a world where such ideals are maintained only at the expense of self-negation and deceit. But to understand the Helmers, their way of life, their conditioning, and the structure of their minds we need to translate our contemporary sensibilities into those of our great-great-grandparents and move into two other countries—the cultural past and the isolated world of provincial Norway in the 1870s. At the center of this world, the presiding spirit of the nineteenth-century "home" is the married wife, the angel in the house, who bears the responsibility for maintaining the virtues of Victorian domesticity: "Household happiness, gracious children, debtless competence, golden mean."[3]

One of the telling ironies of the play is that Torvald, whose very profession as merchant banker depends upon extending credit and loans, is constantly asserting the economic evils of incurring debt: "No debts! Never borrow! There's always something inhibited, something unpleasant, about a home built on credit and borrowed money" (203). His business life and his home life, it would seem, are kept stringently separate, as if the "home" were some inviolate haven against the encroachment of the money ethic on family life, as if the debtless competence of the wife were some compensation for his immersion in the nastiness of daily business. Torvald's "home" is clearly a stronghold of moral virtue, an unsullied alternative to the fallen commercial world, and the responsibility of maintaining its economic cleanliness, its spiritual innocence, falls upon the angel in the house who is very deeply in debt after having forged a signature upon a guarantor's note with blithe indifference to the consequences.

A wife, in 1879, was not legally permitted to borrow without her husband's consent (married women in Norway gained control of their own finances only in 1888), and Nora's economic entanglement in the fallen world of borrowing and debt is occasioned by her inability to raise funds without subterfuge. Whatever her other motives for concealing her loan, she *cannot* go to Torvald without compromising her ideal status in his home. "Debt" is more than a dirty word in his vocabulary; it reverberates with frightful moral condemnation, as it does in Ibsen's Dano-Norwegian original: *gæld* (10), the root word of *gengældelse* (51) or "retribution," the same word Dr. Rank uses for the congenital disease afflicting him. Debt, forgery, and deceit are the realities upon which their comfortable dolls' existence is based, and the angel in the house is a mere hair's breadth removed from her antithesis, the fallen woman who lurks in Torvald's domestic consciousness like a moral leper, tainting the children with her very presence and polluting the home. "A fog of lies like that in a household," he says of such poisoned homes, "and it spreads disease and infection to every part of it. Every breath the children take in that kind of house is reeking with evil germs. . . . Practically all juvenile delinquents come from homes where the mother is dishonest" (233).

The attitudes in the play—moral, economic, gender-based—are (one hopes) no longer current in the middle-class homes that most of us now inhabit, and we have to adjust our notion of the 1990s family as a community of shared interests to the economically dominated unit of the 1870s wherein the values of "home" were morally sanctified at the cost of distorting normal relationships within the family circle. There are other more specific cultural differences, less momentous perhaps than those that relate to nineteenth-century views of "home," "family," and "wife," that nevertheless call for some form of translation. Christmas Eve, in Norway, is the focus of the family's celebration rather than Christmas Day, so it seems in *A Doll's House* that Christmas has been bypassed and the tree disheveled rather prematurely.

There is also, of course, the difficulty of finding equivalents for the various currencies discussed and handled in the play. When Bella proudly proclaims, in the passage quoted above from Dickens's *Our Mutual Friend,* that they enjoy an income of 150 pounds a year, are they considered rich or poor by the standards of 1865? And how are we to evaluate the first gesture that defines Nora's temperament and values in the play?

> NORA: (*To the* PORTER, *taking out her purse*) How much?
>
> PORTER: Fifty *öre.*
>
> NORA: There's a crown. Keep the change. (201)

Is this a gesture of reckless extravagance? a generous seasonal impulse? a confident anticipation of changed economic circumstances? "How much" indeed? The English editor of the Penguin edition unhelpfully annotates 50 *öre* as "the equivalent of a sixpence"[4]—a coin no longer current in the realm. Taking inflation into account, this might seem a negligible amount to puzzle over, but the important point of the exchange is that Nora tips the porter an amount equivalent to the cost of his services: a tip of 100 percent. What was the purchasing power of 50 *öre* in the Norway of 1879, and how much time might Nora have to spend on copy work to earn the money she casually disburses as small change? A small coin can be a large tip for a woman in her position, and yet it cannot be said of Nora that she does not know the value of money. The actress must find the precise nature of the subtextual motive for Nora's initial gesture, and the reader-as-director must *translate* it into a revelation of her character.

LANGUAGE OF THE EVERYDAY AND THE SUBLIME

Language, however, remains the great stumbling block of translation—especially when the easy colloquial style of the original congeals into the stilted phrasing of an alien tongue, and the economical and concrete word blocks of the Norwegian language trail off into the vague and periphrastic abstractions of English equivalents. When, for instance, Dr. Rank speaks of his impending death and the cruel injustice of a world where inherited disease wreaks its retribution on family life, Nora puts her hands over her ears and cries out "*Sniksnak! Lystig; lystig!*" (51). Her language is full of everyday expletives like *pyt* and *sniksnak*, the chatter of the nursery, perhaps, as untranslatable as the little verbal tics of English or North American colloquial speech. "And don't say 'gee,'" Willy Loman tells his son in *Death of a Salesman*,[5] embarrassed by the utterances of immaturity in the world of big business. The problem of shifting "gee" into Norwegian is comparable, I should imagine, to that of shifting "*sniksnak*" into English: there is no substantive content to either word. Einar Haugen's dictionary provides "fiddle-faddle" (tonally appropriate in its silliness, but unutterable on the modern stage), which is understood as "nonsense" (Archer, 81) or "rubbish" (245). What we need to hear are the childish tonalities of Nora's response to death and disease, her tendency to deflect their implications into the realm of the nursery where such horrors become unthinkable. "*Sniksnak*" is not merely a grotesquely inappropriate rejoinder (underscored by the evasive gesture of blocking the ears), but the language of a woman who *refuses* to contemplate a reality too appallingly close to home. It is not primarily a rebuke of "Nonsense!" to Dr. Rank. It is one of the little clucking noises of a child desperately trying to console herself in the face of her own secret fears with a sort of verbal macaroon. *Tonality,* and not the literal content of the words she uses, is the clue to Nora's character, and this is the one essential quality of language that most firmly resists translation.

"*Lystig; lystig!*" presents problems of its own. Ibsen's first English translator, Henrietta Frances Lord, hears this as an injunction to Dr. Rank: "Do be funny, funny."[6] Archer offers typically Edwardian encouragement, "Now cheer up!" and most translators follow suit. Again, it seems to me that "*lystig*" is not an attempt to impose cheerfulness on the deeply depressed Dr. Rank but rather an attempt to invoke an already forfeited element of merriment in the dolls' home, to reinvoke the lost spirit of gaiety in the darkening room. The word represents the quintessential mood of dollydom, the veneer of false contentment spread thinly over the marriage and the Helmers' entire, unthinking way of life.

"*Lystig*" belongs, with "*sniksnak*," to the lexicon of self-deceiving and evasive verbal ploys that deny the reality of an emotional experience for which Nora cannot find the appropriate language. This becomes manifestly clear toward the end of the play when Nora *must* find the words that define her existentially, when the adequacy of "*lystighet*"—cheerfulness—is finally summed up and dismissed as a state of inauthentic being in the real world. She must leave the dolls' house, Nora tells Torvald, because it fails to sustain her spiritually, because she sees beyond its superficial nursery satisfactions. In the original text, Ibsen chooses his terms with meticulous care:

> HELMER: *Har du ikke været lykkelig her?*
> NORA: *Nej, det har jeg aldrig været. Jeg trode det; men jeg har aldrig været det.*
> HELMER: *Ikke—ikke lykkelig!*
> NORA: *Nej; bare lystig.* (83)

The Oxford Ibsen provides the following translation:

> HELMER: Haven't you been happy here?
> NORA: No, never. I thought I was, but I wasn't really.
> HELMER: Not . . . not happy!
> NORA: No, just gay. (280)

The difference between "happy" and "gay"—"*lykkelig*" and "*lystig*"—may seem rather slight, but the architectonic word structure of the play should alert us to the peculiar nature of a language in search of adequate expression for subtle shades of feeling and the varying intensities of the emotional life.

Part of Nora's difficulty (perhaps Ibsen's) is that there is no definitive nineteenth-century vocabulary in which to define the existential or psychological states that have become commonplace in modern discourse. Nora, anxious to be properly understood, must invoke various gradations of feeling in order to distinguish profound spiritual satisfaction in her marriage from the mere appearance of domestic bliss. "*Lykkelig*" and "*lystig*" are not synonymous, as they appear to be in English translation, and Nora is trying to distinguish between "being happy" and "having fun"—that is, between a spiritual condition and a moment of pleasure, between existential delight and temporary gratification. "*Lykkelig*" with its connotations of good fortune ("luck") I take to refer to a state of well-being. "*Lystig*" with its connotations of inclination and desire ("lust") I take to refer to a bout of sporadic elation. Words, in *A Doll's House,* evolve their meanings so that even the most casual colloquialism finally modulates into a term that is part of a complex value system.

"*Ikke—ikke lykkelig!*" "Not—not happy!" Torvald exclaims, and his tone of incredulity and incomprehension alerts us immediately to the peculiarly Ibsenian sense of two languages being spoken simultaneously: the everyday and the existential, the public and the esoteric, the known and the inexplicable. The same word may carry profoundly different meanings, especially when the meaning intended by the speaker is at obvious variance with the meaning received by the listener. There are typical moments in Ibsen's drama when this failure of translation occurs, when the clichés of everyday expression suddenly resonate with an unutterable meaning that no one seems to understand. Translation, in these contexts, is not merely a matter of finding an appropriate English term but a matter of recognizing the unspoken within the spoken, the mystical within the matter of fact. Take, for example, this brief interchange between Nora and Mrs. Linde in act 2:

> NORA: *Det er jo det vidunderlige, som nu vil ske.*
>
> FRU LINDE: *Det vidunderlige?*
>
> NORA: *Ja, det vidunderlige. Men det er så forfærdeligt, Kristine;*
> *det må ikke ske.*(60)

NORA: You see something miraculous is going to happen.

MRS LINDE: Something miraculous?

NORA: Yes, a miracle. But something so terrible as well, Kristine—oh, it must *never* happen. (256)

Nearly all translators, from the time of Archer onward, regard "*det vidunderlige*" as "a miracle"—a key concept in the play, and one of its iterative and insistent ideas. It is, moreover, a term perfectly in keeping with the Christmas season and its reminder of the Christian miracle. "*Det vidunderlige*" resonates with a mystical and pseudoreligious emotion quite consistent with Nora's romantic yearning, but there is something clangingly symbolic about the word in translation, as if Ibsen were alerting us to thematic significance. Nothing could be deadlier in performance than a Nora who speaks of "the miraculous" in this semaphoric and overtranslated manner.

Nora uses the same word that she has casually uttered on at least six different occasions in act 1—"*Å, det er vidunderligt!*" (13), "*Å, ja, ja, det er rigtignok vidunderligt at leve og være lykkelig!*" (23), and so on. It is a simple, colloquial expression of pleasure and delight: "Oh, it's marvellous" (206), "Oh yes! When you're happy, life is a wonderful thing!" (216). Unembarrassed, Ibsen uses the identical term over and over again, unconcerned with synonyms or the need to vary his vocabulary, and repetition accrues meaning like a snowball, until the most ordinary of everyday expressions become invested with overtones of the extraordinary. There is no need to overstate Nora's private lexicon of meanings in symbolic language, and the translator's challenge is to find the poetic within the banal and to permit the transformation of direct and realistic speech into heightened meaning without rhetorical decoration. The model for this form of poetry is not Shakespeare with his extraordinary range of terms and profusion of images, but rather Racine, the master of minimalist poetry whose language is scaled down to an irreducible sufficiency of terms, whose every concept grows from context to context until its meaning begins to echo the unspoken poetry of the inner life. In the Dano-Norwegian original, "*det vidunderlige*" may indeed modulate into a vision of the miraculous, but Nora's translation of the colloquial into the romantic-religious remains profoundly esoteric and mysterious. *She* knows what she means when she speaks this ordinary phrase, even if Mrs. Linde is left perplexed. The wonderful thing is also a terrifying thing: it is both miracle and martyrdom, supreme wonder and supreme sacrifice, the inexplicable something for which one waits in hope and expectation and dread. But there is surely a great gap between what is marvelous in life and what is miraculous, and by the time we arrive at the end of act 2, "*det vidunderlige*" has begun to resonate with greater wonders than everyday life could possibly accommodate. The most successful translation is one that will envelop Nora's imagined "miracle" in layers of irony that reveal the tonalities of romantic impossibility within simple colloquial phrasing.

In act 1, "*det vidunderlige*" is a notation for the wonderful happiness of having a nice, safe job, a good, fat income, and the opportunity for upward mobility (206). In act 2, it transcends the coziness of dolls' house values and strains towards the heights of romantic wish-dreams of heroic male sacrifice and wifely self-immolation. At the end of act 3 the ideal disintegrates and "*det vidunderlige*" lies shattered and discredited. Nora has waited patiently for eight years for Torvald's transfiguration, but her dolls' house husband does not behave like the chivalric hero of romantic novels. On the contrary. He abuses her in a shameful display of petulance, betraying her most basic hope of emotional support. The most wonderful thing of all, "*det vidunderligste*" (88), should really be the most ordinary of human expectations. The meaning that Nora confers on "the miraculous" finally turns out to be a "real marriage" based not on romantic fantasy but on respect, support, decency, and care.

NORA: *Ak, Torvald, da måtte det vidunderligste ske.—*

HELMER: *Nævn mig dette vidunderligste!*

NORA: *Da måtte både du og jeg forvandle os således at—. Å, Torvald, jeg tror ikke længer på noget vidunderligt.*

HELMER: *Men jeg vil tro på det. Nævn det! Forvandle os således at—?*

NORA: *At samliv mellem os to kunde bli et ægteskab.* (88)

NORA: Ah, Torvald, only by a miracle of miracles . . .
HELMER: Name it, this miracle of miracles!
NORA: Both you and I would have to change to the point
where . . . Oh, Torvald, I don't believe in miracles anymore.
HELMER: But I *will* believe. Name it! Change to the point
where . . . ?
NORA: Where we could make a real marriage of our lives together.
(286)

The most wonderful thing of all, the "miracle of miracles," is no longer the myth of heroic sacrifice, nor is it the virgin birth in Bethlehem. Neither romance nor religion claim the ardent faith of the Helmers, instead they hold a tenuous belief in human beings' capacity to change the circumstances of their being and the quality of their spiritual life. The wonder inheres in man and woman as creatures in command of their own existential well-being. Redefined in this way, the miraculous now lies within their grasp, not as an ideal, but as a reality: they have the power to transform themselves from dolls into human beings of flesh and blood, and so restructure the nature of a mere "coupling" into a genuine "marriage." The last line of the play is Torvald's, spoken with an onrush of hope: "*Det vidunderligste—?*" And the play ends with the husband's open-ended question and the door slamming on the dolls' house as the wife emerges into a world of change and difficult self-transformation.

The nature of Ibsen's "poetry," then, is the reiterated use of key concepts that undergo a remarkable metamorphosis of meaning evolving from the chitchat of ordinary speech to a newly defined notation of our existential being. The challenge to the translator is to reveal the heightened overtones in the ordinary phrase without resorting to the sort of old high Ibsenese that makes his language unspeakable. As English readers of an archaic Norwegian text we need, at least, to be aware of the peculiarities of Ibsen's realistic prose style and not mistake the tip of a translator's iceberg for the totality of the play's submerged meanings.

Translating Et Dukkehjem into A Doll's House

THE SECOND-PERSON PRONOUN

There are, as well, more specific examples of Dano-Norwegian grammatical peculiarity that English translation cannot reproduce, and that reveal the little psychopathologies of Ibsen's ordinary middle-class protagonists. Torvald, for example, bears a grudge against Krogstad that is so pathetically small-minded in the original text that Nora dares to criticize him for it. In the Oxford Ibsen Torvald explains his attitude in a clumsy, periphrastic way: "There's no reason why you shouldn't know we were once on terms of some familiarity. And he in his tactless way, makes no attempt to hide the fact, particularly when other people are present. On the contrary, he thinks he has every right to treat me as an equal, with his 'Torvald this' and 'Torvald that' every time he opens his mouth. I find it extremely irritating, I can tell you. He would make my position at the Bank absolutely intolerable" (242–43). In the English text it sounds as if Torvald is reacting to tactless insubordination, Krogstad calling the boss by name.

In Ibsen's original, Torvald's extreme irritation is grounded upon two small phrases: "*vi er dus*," "*du, du Helmer*" (48). Krogstad, it transpires, simply uses the wrong second-person pronoun. His "terms of some familiarity" really means that he addresses Torvald as "*du*" instead of "*De*," just as in French one might allow one's tongue to slip from the formal "*vous*" to the informal "*tu*" in social conversation. It is not even a matter of 'Torvald this' or 'Torvald that.' Simply a slight adjustment in forms of address makes Torvald's position so absolutely intolerable, and on such grounds he is prepared to dismiss the man from his position at the bank and render him once more destitute. Nora precipitates disaster by calling her husband "*smålig*," "petty" or "narrow-minded." But Torvald's shallowness, his social pretension, and his pusillanimity appear all the more heinous in Dano-Norwegian because a man's fate depends on his grammar. Torvald is more thoroughly discredited in the original than he could possibly be in a language that draws no nice distinctions between different forms of the second-person pronoun—unless we endorse Archer's archaic rendering of "*vi er dus*" as "we say 'thou' to each other."[7]

37

FORBIDDEN LANGUAGE

What do we make of Nora's desire to shatter the propriety of the dolls' house by cursing like a trooper in the living room? What word could she use that will detonate in the modern world with the same shocking force that it had in 1879? She wants to exercise the man's prerogative—this, ostensibly, is what she has in mind. "I would simply love to say: 'Damn'" (220), she announces with the same innocuous effect that Eliza Doolittle's "Not bloody likely!" now has on an audience. But Ibsen's phrase goes right to the heart of the matter. "*Jeg har sådan en umådelig lyst til at sige: død og pine*," says the Dano-Norwegian Nora (27). She has a compelling urge to cry out: "Death and pain!"—expressing not merely the abstract concept of damnation but also the appalling reality of what she is suffering in the decorous silence imposed on her by the dolls' house. The oath, in 1879, elicits shock from those who hear her. (We need, again, to imagine a sensibility that is outraged by such a curse.) But more than this, more than the need to exercise a man's prerogative or violate the good taste of the bourgeois parlor, Nora must find a way of expressing the anguish and desolation beneath her "gay" exterior. The contrast between her crunching on macaroons to sweeten her existence and the reality of that existence is perfectly conveyed in her irresistible need to cry out "*død og pine*"; for however mild her oath may seem, the sense of suffering lurking beneath innocuous surfaces is everywhere apparent in the play. And if propriety forbids her cursing in the dolls' house, then Nora's only recourse is to *perform* the hidden torments of the psychic life. "*Død og pine*" is, in turn, *translated* into action when Nora dances the frenetic tarantella—the perfect correlative to what may not honestly be uttered in her marriage.

• • •

The greatest consolation to those of us who have to take translations on trust and acknowledge a measure of poetic loss in the words is that Ibsen's characters *demand* to be thoroughly understood because Ibsen has translated their deepest concerns and most esoteric ideas into strong dramatic action. Character is revealed not only in the semiotics of language but in the semiotics of theater, in performance, with its close correlation of verbal metaphor with visual metaphor, its conjunction of word and gesture, its *enactment* of ideas, and its revelation of character through everyday objects invested with extraordinary meaning. Nora tips the porter. Nora dresses in her Capri fishergirl's fancy dress. Nora dances. Nora tantalizes Rank with her flesh-colored stockings. Nora tinsels the Christmas tree. The play is a subtle verbal construct in which the multiple transformations of a word like "*vidunderlig*" underscore the transformations of mind and spirit in the protagonist, but it also contains a series of actions and events in which meaning is conveyed through symbols and music and body language and costume—in other words, through all the nonverbal resources of the theater that are standard in all cultures and do not require translation. It is in Ibsen's stagecraft that the deeply submerged meaning is made articulate through the poetry of the theater itself.

5

Visual Metaphors and Performance

LIGHTS

A Doll's House was written in 1879, the same year in which the theater took a quantum leap in technological sophistication. Edison's incandescent bulb not only illuminated the stage with greater brilliance than ever before but focused direction, varied the intensity of light, and transformed the stage from a reflecting mirror into an atmospheric lamp.

A Doll's House (as if anticipating this revolution in stagecraft) makes constant and subtle demands of the lighting designer who must provide an emotional context for the language spoken and underscore the dialogue in a counterpoint more delicate than the sonorous musical accompaniment of the old melodrama. In act 2, for example, the crucial scene in which Nora dallies with Dr. Rank is prefaced with a stage direction: "*During what follows it begins to grow dark*" (244). Within the context of this crepuscular light Nora's dialogue of strained levity, provocative sexual wheedling, moral miscalculation, and sudden recantation takes place. At the end of this appallingly embarrassing scene Nora calls for a lamp, and the dramatic effect is the restoration of the dolls' house atmosphere of cheery normality. But the brightness also underscores Nora's moment of illumination in which her sexual power play as a doll is revealed in all its crudity and in which the comforting illusions of the darkness are dissipated by her acute self-consciousness of moral temperament. This is one of Ibsen's brilliant visual moments, projected and controlled in performance by the technical resources of the theater. To recreate this onstage effect—the depressing gloom that envelops the awful cheeriness of Nora's seduction scene, her sudden insight into the ugliness of dollydom, and her pique when her old romantic assumptions collapse—readers of Ibsen's text must become their own lighting designers and envision the effect on some mental stage. What is *said* is inseparable from the light in which it is *seen*.

SETTING

Language in the theater is enhanced by a complex system of visual and auditory codes, and meaning often moves beyond the spoken metaphor as if projected through all the technical resources of the stage. To grasp the full meaning, we must become not only our own lighting technician but our own director, designer of set and costumes, choreographer, properties person, and musician. Ibsen's realism makes extraordinary demands of the reader. It reflects the mundane surfaces of the humdrum, bourgeois parlor—a world of lamps and sofas and tiled stoves and cabinets filled with bric-a-brac and Christmas trees and all the solid objects of our day-to-day existence. But, like the colloquial ordinariness of Ibsen's language that begins to reverberate with unspoken echoes, these surfaces suddenly reveal unexpected depths.

Many critics have detected a quality in Ibsen's stagecraft: he transforms the stage from mirror into lamp, from a world that merely reflects the quality of middle-class existence into a luminous revelation of the invisible forces behind the phenomenal world. The bourgeois parlor remains a bourgeois parlor, as Virginia Woolf remarks of

Ibsen's illuminating style, but, at the same time, "the paraphernalia of reality have at certain moments to become the veil through which we can see infinity."[1]

Most remarkable about Ibsen's stagecraft is its ability to expand the bourgeois parlor, as it were, into an everywhere and make it resonate with the significance of those abstract spaces in Greek and Shakespearean theater. The most archaic of rituals—the Dionysian dithyramb or the choral dance—reenter the domestic world of the dolls' house and, without anachronism, reveal the contours of the universal amphitheater within the boxed-in, trapped existence of the nineteenth-century set. Ibsen gives us a hard-edged, solid world: a sense of the compartmentalized lives of modern urban living dominated by doors, onstage and off, that shut in fantasies and shut out reality, that isolate a community of domestic strangers and insulate them against the cold and forbidding world outside that is their only alternative to the constricted doll's house way of life. This is Nora's "home" and Ibsen insists, in his stage directions, that it be *"hyggeligt og smagfuldt"* (9); "comfortable and tastefully appointed," with pleasant furniture, pictures, china figurines, attractively bound books, and a cheery fire in the porcelain stove. But some spaces are sacrosanct (like Torvald's study, which is an extension of his banker's office), some doors may not be opened with impunity, nor is there free access to the letter box, which is kept under lock and key. Some modern set designers have chosen to take Ibsen's ambiguous image of the dolls' house world and emphasize the metaphor concealed beneath its superficial coziness: a prison with a row of 18 cell-like doors, a deconstructed box set, or a psychological construct as insubstantial as a paper cutout house held together only by consent.[2] But Ibsen asks us to see both images simultaneously as a single, visual *tvertimod*: the comfortable home and the suffocating prison, both Eden and anti-Eden, a solid world of social realities but also an "idea" to which Nora gives credence and that she can annihilate by withdrawing her acquiescence, leaving by the same door through which she had first entered. The curtain rises on Nora ringing the front doorbell to be ushered through two doors into her world of Christmas cheer. It falls as she slams the front door on a devastated world, its *"lystighet"* annihilated by a clarification of consciousness and an alteration in her angle of moral vision. Nora's transformation is inseparable from the radical transformation of the dolls' house itself, despite the apparently indomitable solidity of the realistic nineteenth-century box set.

The "infinity" to which we gain access through the stagecraft of *A Doll's House* is the boundless world of Nora's psychic nature, what Ibsen understood in the vocabulary of his day as "*det ubevidste sjæleliv*"; "the mysterious life of the subconscious mind," with its heights of moral self-awareness and its depths of self-deception. We "know" Nora not only as the romantic poet of the miracle but as the woman who dresses and dances and who stands most articulately revealed as a frenzied maenad, draped in a gaudy shawl, banging a tambourine and whirling out of control, her hair tumbling round her shoulders. The elements composing the climactic moment in the play—the decorously crafted dolls' house world of bourgeois propriety that is split apart by madness, the Neapolitan garment that unleashes a hot Mediterranean sensuality into the cold Scandinavian wintertime, the anguished body language that breaks out of the controlled rhythms of the music and beats out its own wild dithyramb—depend on all the technical resources of the theater, and all these elements fuse into an image of Nora's *totentanz,* an enacted metaphor of death and torment that transforms an ethnic dance into an emblem of the "*sjæleliv.*"

COSTUME

Character is most obviously extended onstage through what actors wear, and Ibsen is very specific about dress. Dress establishes, in an instant, a range of information about the character on the stage: social position, psychological state, economic status. Mrs. Linde, for example, establishes her presence even before she begins to speak in her diffident and embarrassed way. She enters, writes Ibsen, "*i rejsetoj*" (14); "in clothes suitable for travel." Perhaps we no longer register the significance of her dress because in our age travel is unremarkable and habitual. But a nineteenth-century audience would recognize at once the theatrical signs of transience, displacement, and impermanence that make Mrs. Linde the dialectical antithesis of the doll comfortably ensconced in her dolls' house. Her clothes are perfectly suited to her subdued, unhappy manner, and, when she speaks of her life, the visual projection of a displaced woman is reinforced by Mrs. Linde's sense of terrible loneliness. She sees herself as socially redundant, a spare part, a useless and lost creature for whom there is no place in the world outside the dolls' house.

The initial impression of Mrs. Linde is important, all the more so when the structure of the play emphasizes an interchange of roles: in the last act of *A Doll's House* Mrs. Linde discovers a secure place in the world and her vocation as wife and mother, whereas Nora leaves her comfortable home to endure the insecurity of displacement, loneliness, and bereavement. Nora leaves, in other words, wearing the same type of clothing Mrs. Linde had worn when she entered, having almost literally transformed herself from doll into traveler through a series of costume changes. First she strips away the Neapolitan fancy dress—the fishergirl's costume from Capri—and reenters in her ordinary everyday things. Then she clothes herself in "*ydertoj*" (87)—a winter overcoat and a hat—finally pulling around her shoulders the large black shawl that remains from her fancy dress and transforming herself into a living emblem of the tragedy that has befallen the doll-wife and doll-mother. And then she leaves with her "*vadsæk*" (88), a small travelling bag containing the sum total of her possessions. Even the costume design in *A Doll's House* establishes a perfect architectonic system of meanings and existential states.

No single piece of clothing, however, captures the spirit of the doll more stunningly than Nora's Neapolitan fishergirl fancy dress, purchased during the couple's sojourn in Capri. We learn from snatches of dialogue that Torvald is rather fond of having Nora amuse him in the evenings by dressing up and dancing and reciting (215). One of the roles of the doll in the dolls' house is to "play" and (one assumes) to titillate. We also gather that Nora "plays" with very conscious intention, and that in dressing up and dancing she is exercising the only form of power available to the doll in the dolls' house: the power of sexual manipulation, the power of some northern Lysistrata. She knows how dollydom operates and that sex alone guarantees her position in the household and gets her what she wants. So she acts the sexual doll, even to the extent of allowing Torvald to choose the costume and the dance that most reveal the hoydenish mistress beneath the angel in the house. The fancy dress from Capri is all sex and sensuality, southern passion in a northern clime, a dressing up device that transforms Nora into the kind of ethnic doll in the plastic container found in most international souvenir shops. The costume represents the *form* of her marital existence, the external *shape* of her role as a living sexual fantasy in the bourgeois bedroom. (This much is clear in the last act, when Torvald hurries her home from the party, sexually aroused by her dance and anxious to get her into bed.) But the Neapolitan fishergirl outfit is more than a source of male titillation and female power in the dolls' house. It is also the play's most articulate symbol of the illusions on which the doll life thrives.

We see Nora playing the doll game in act 1, giving Torvald the impression, at any rate, that he controls her and chooses her costume for the Christmas party at the Stenborgs. This is the first stage of the sexual turn-on:

NORA: (*Still leaning against the back of the chair, running her fingers through his hair.*) If you hadn't been so busy, Torvald, I'd have asked you to do me an awfully big favour.

HELMER: Let me hear it. What's it to be?

NORA: Nobody's got such good taste as you. And the thing is I do so want to look my best at the fancy dress ball. Torvald, couldn't you give me some advice and tell me what you think I ought to go as, and how I should arrange my costume?

HELMER: Aha! So my impulsive little woman is asking for somebody to come to her rescue, eh?

NORA: Please, Torvald, I never get anywhere without your help. (232)

Nora hopes the payback for *allowing* Torvald to manipulate her as a doll will be Krogstad's reinstatement at the bank. This is a reasonable assumption, for Torvald finds her irresistible in the costume he has had specially made for her in Capri.

We see the various bits and pieces of this costume throughout act 2, together with the two shawls that go with the dress—the gaudy colored shawl and the black one, and in act 3 Nora appears elaborately dressed up in the outfit, before finally discarding the thing for her travelling clothes. The costume makes its first appearance at the beginning of act 2, enclosed in a large cardboard box, just as the bright world of the dolls' house begins to gutter like the burnt out stumps of candles on the bedraggled Christmas tree, and Nora's attitude towards her tattered fancy dress is the first small indication of her revulsion against the humiliating sexual game playing, the pretense of petty domestic power, and the illusions of dollydom that the dress comes to represent for her: "Oh, if only I could rip them up into a thousand pieces!" she cries (235). All the fancy dress needs, however, is Mrs. Linde's skill with needle and thread to restore it to its former glory and, because Torvald cannot endure the sight of domestic business, she takes the costume off to mend it, leaving behind only the gaudy shawl and the flesh-colored silk stockings, visual reminders of the Neapolitan fantasy and the sexually provocative implications of "dressing up."

Again, we have to think ourselves into 1879 when the legs of pianos in some middle-class parlors were modestly draped against embarrassment. (Even 30 years later, the mere mention of a female undergarment in Synge's *Playboy of the Western World* was enough to cause rioting in the theaters of Ireland and the United States.) Now, in the blasé world of Maidenform advertisements and lingerie displays in shop windows it requires a leap of the prurient imagination to recreate the impact of Nora's flesh-colored stockings on the susceptible Dr. Rank. The scene with Dr. Rank is distasteful, not merely because Nora practices the wiles of feminine seduction on her husband's best friend, nor because she teases the dying man by cruelly arousing his desire. Her behavior is meretricious because she uses sexuality as a trade-off for money, because this is her habitual means of getting what she wants. In this instance, she needs enough cash to buy back her bond from Krogstad. It is a last-ditch effort to extricate herself from a deadly situation, and the measure of her desperation is matched only by the perversity of her sexual maneuver in the darkening parlor:

NORA: Come here, Dr. Rank. I want to show you something.

RANK: (*sits.*) What is it?

NORA: Look!

RANK: Silk stockings.

NORA: Flesh-coloured! Aren't they lovely! Of course, it's dark here now, but tomorrow. . . . No, no, no, you can only look at the feet. Oh well, you might as well see a bit higher up, too.

RANK: Hmm. . . .

NORA: Why are you looking so critical? Don't you think they'll fit?

RANK: I couldn't possibly offer any informed opinion about that.

NORA: (*looks at him for a moment.*) Shame on you. (*Hits him lightly across the ear with the stockings.*) Take that! (247)

The stockings—both clothing and hand prop—resonate with an obscenity quite distinct from their innocuous reality. They become the channel (as it were) for a discharge of sexual energy that Nora carelessly unleashes but that she cannot finally control. Rank, provoked into a false sense of intimacy by Nora's patent sexual advances, declares his great love for her—his willingness to die for her—and suddenly the situation becomes intolerable for Nora. Her body tenses slightly, there is a typically understated moment of epiphany: "Ah," she says, quietly, and then with great self-possession she calls for the light.

SUBTEXT AND MOTIVATION

At this moment in Ibsen's play the meaning of the text is almost exclusively at the disposal of the actress, and the subtext demands a clarity of performance to realize the complexity of Nora's revelation.

The reader, as director, must infer the quality of her "*sjæleliv*" in the modulation of tone from erotic titillation, to the coy wheedling of a favor, to the unspoken perception that saddens her and leads her to cry for the lamp. At this point, Nora can get whatever she wants from Rank, and with success in the very palm of her hand she suddenly relinquishes her major objective in the scene and consigns herself to the dreadful inevitability of giving in to Krogstad's threats. She displays a moment of extraordinary moral courage in the face of adversity, a determination to suffer the consequences of her actions rather than pursue the doll game to its assured victorious conclusion.

Motive, clearly, must be inferred from a set of extremely oblique directions in the text: *stiffening slightly, sadly, rises and speaks evenly and calmly* (248–49), which are the residue of nineteenth-century melodramatic gesture, now controlled and understated and realigned to the noncommittal style of the realistic theater. John Northam reads these notations as a heroic leap of the moral conscience: "It is the spoilt Nora who does the flirting—it is the heroic woman underneath, the woman of fundamentally sound principles who puts a stop to the nonsense when it begins to offend her sense of rightness."[3] Northam's reading is a perfectly feasible directorial note to the actress, and Nora's character is stamped with a particular kind of meaning by playing the scene in this way. But these Ibsenian moments are dense with possibility, and there is no comprehensive subtext that subsumes all meaning in a single performance. Moral shame, embarrassment, a sense (perhaps) of having violated decent conduct by begging money from one who declares himself your lover, of having compromised integrity by *using* sexuality in the manner of a whore, all these possibilities are implicit in John Northam's reading of the scene.

In summoning the light Nora might very possibly be acknowledging the shameful reality of the doll's situation with the moral insight of the transformed woman, but another subtextual revelation must surely reveal the sudden disintegration of her most cherished illusion of the dolls' house male. For just as Torvald is cast in the romantic role of the chivalric Savior, so Dr. Rank has become the phantom sugar daddy of her reveries, the subject of her dreams of economic salvation and one of the dolls' house illusions that she shares, half jokingly and half seriously, with Mrs. Linde: "I used to sit here and pretend that some rich old gentlemen had fallen in love with me. . . . and that now he had died, and when they opened his will, there in big letters were the words: 'My entire fortune is to be paid over, immediately and in cash, to charming Mrs. Nora Helmer'" (216). In the scene with the stockings she has been treating Dr. Rank not as a dearly loved and respected friend, but as the cliché of her fantasies—a male doll whose death is merely a playful convenience, a source of funding. Her behavior has consistently ignored the human content of their interchange, consistently failed to acknowledge the reality of Rank's terminal condition. Her illusion of the male doll is as humiliating as the doll role she has trained herself to play.

When Rank declares his love for her, the shame of her dalliance is surely complicated by an awareness of her own Bovaryism, the tendency to reduce living substance to the empty forms of perverse fantasy. Rank demands to be seen in all his pathetic and suffering reality, and with his claim upon her serious attention, he spoils the dream on which her doll's existence thrives. "Oh!" she says, sadly. And the actress must read into the noncommittal sigh a world of unspoken meanings before Nora reproaches Dr. Rank for spoiling her illusion forever. "With calm self-discipline"—*jævnt og roligt* (54)—she calls for the light, and then, rather like Hedda Gabler after her determination to die for what she most values, she reconciles herself to reality and relaxes into the inevitability of a decision firmly taken. Now she can smile at Rank and tease him once again. Her moral courage is undeniable. But her moment of ethical heroism coexists with the awful sense of deprivation she experiences, self-revealed in the lamp light: she loses the comfortable dolls' house world in which truths remain unspoken and dolls are not normally called upon to sit in judgment over the self. Refusing to extricate herself from the terror of her situation by the morally disgusting means of the doll's house and finally confronting the truth of Dr. Rank's condition as a mirror of her own inevitable fate, Nora arrives at a frightening conclusion: the opposite of dollydom, for her, is death.

Death, for Nora, is the only way out of her predicament. This much seems clear in the moment of calm determination in the lamplight. Fate requires that she is pushed to the brink of her resolve by the relentlessness of circumstance. Incapable now of turning to Rank for help and contemptuous of the dolls' house techniques of extrication, Nora is finally brought to the brink by Krogstad's desperation. Hammer blow by hammer blow, he smashes all hope of an alternative solution. No, he will not relent. No, he will not return the IOU even for cash in hand. No, he will not be bought off for a higher sum. No, he will not be deterred by empty threats of suicide. Pampered bourgeois dolls, he scoffs, don't do that sort of thing, and they are not capable of confronting the ugly, bloated fact of a death beneath the ice.

But what people choose to do depends on the extent of their courage—that same quality of "*mod*" (59) that Nora shares with Hedda Gabler—and Krogstad's image of the dredged up corpse has the effect of clarifying Nora's intention, of shifting her notion of a vaguely conceived redemptive impulse to acknowledging the inescapable reality of physical decay. She must find the courage to face this horror and an equal measure of courage to acknowledge that even suicide will not save the situation: Krogstad will not hesitate to compromise her after death nor spare Torvald the truth about her crime. But her tragedy is no longer one of mere public exposure because she has offended her husband, flouted the moral code of his house, placed him in the power of a subordinate with grandiose ambitions of running the bank, compromised his honor and defiled it. However exaggerated her sense of the situation, however narrowly defined by the residual romanticism of her dolls' house image of Torvald or her acceptance of the moral ethos of the community, Nora's mounting fear is real and terrifying. She *must* die. Her death will be conclusive proof of her blame, conclusive evidence in the face of Torvald's "miraculous" assumption of responsibility of her moral delinquency. The pathos of Nora's desperate situation is enveloped in irony as the self-styled tragedienne forestalls the moment of death with her penultimate dolly performance.

The full horror of Nora's revelation expresses itself in a peculiarly

"Greek" moment in *A Doll's House*: Nora dances. Once again, Ibsen's dramatic method translates idea into action, language into enacted metaphors of the heroine's "soul life," projecting meaning simultaneously through all the resources of the theater: gesture, music, costume, symbolic movement, words. And all the disparate images of the dolls' house marriage suddenly coalesce in a single, highly ambiguous theatrical statement. After the calm and clarifying moment of illumination with Rank, this reversion to the manipulative ploys of dollydom seems a contradiction of the leap forward in moral intelligence and tragic self-awareness. Nora begins to sound like the doll-wife for which Torvald has consistently mistaken her, the minx who shamelessly flatters the masculine ego of those on whom she practices her guile: "I shan't be able to dance tomorrow if I don't rehearse it with you. . . . Come and sit here and play for me, Torvald dear. Tell me what to do, keep me right—as you always do" (258). But a new tone seems to have crept into these self-abnegating phrases, an ironic echo of what she has been told, how she has been treated, a summing-up of the attitudes that define the woman's role in the dolls' house. What distinguishes Nora, now, is her self-consciousness, her grasp upon the nature of role-playing, and her understanding of the way in which both behavior and language are conditioned by the expectations of the male-centered world. Nora, as Inga-Stina Ewbank has shown, speaks with the sort of female helplessness that her husband expects of her when she speaks to *him*—although she has a different idiom when she speaks to Mrs. Linde, or when she speaks in "lonely agony" with a voice of her own. "Nora is a living . . . proof," writes Dr. Ewbank, "of the point maintained by many modern sociolinguists: that women have to be bilingual in a male society."[4] An irony has now entered her discourse, and it soon becomes apparent that her concessions to Torvald's control are countermanded by an intensity of emotional need that he cannot comprehend—any more than he can grasp the meaning of Nora's body language, the third of many languages she speaks, as it cries out in an agony of suddenly unrepressed suffering.

She drapes herself in the long gaudy shawl of the Capri costume, snatches up the tambourine, and almost instantly begins to whirl completely beyond the rhythmic control of Torvald's piano. Wildness, hysteria possesses her. Torvald gives the piano up to Dr. Rank and tries to choreograph her movements, but the ferocity intensifies, her hair falls disheveled about her shoulders, and the bystanders stand spellbound as if in the presence of a frenzied maenad. "You are dancing as though your life depended upon it," says Torvald (259). His platitude suddenly resonates with a meaning he cannot possibly grasp: he has hit on the awful reality of the death for which she is gearing herself, and the symbolic danse macabre implicit in the Neapolitan tarantella—the dance of the victim of the tarantula spider, and the delirious attempt of the body to rid itself of the poison. This is not the customary sexual titillation that Torvald has come to expect of Nora's performance. This dance is her struggle for life, a swallowing and a spitting out of death in an act that projects its horror in the very process of transcending it. Above all, it is a great transformative mystery, a metamorphosis of the quaint Neapolitan doll into the suffering woman, and an exposure of the "*død og pine*" (27)—"the death and the pain"—beneath the pretty role-playing of domestic dollydom. Poison and antidote are simultaneously present in Nora's tarantella as she deconstructs the illusions on which the Helmer marriage thrives in the very act of incarnating them.

The Dancing Doll

Ibsen's image of the dancing doll is a complex, many layered visual metaphor with a history that looks back to women as the sexual playthings of early nineteenth-century romanticism and forward to the postromantic automata of male erotic fantasies. While Ibsen was working on *A Doll's House,* Jacques Offenbach was in the process of composing his opéra comique, *The Tales of Hoffmann,* based on some of E. T. A. Hoffmann's stories of frustrated love, one of which tells of his love for Olympia, the paragon of womanly perfection whose language is limited to "yes" and whose very presence is an invitation to carnal surrender. No matter that Olympia's coloratura singing is somewhat mechanical, or that her dancing whirls out of control. The spectacles through which Hoffmann is obliged to view this miraculous automaton blind him to reality, until the moment when his blinkered view of woman's sexuality is shattered by the breaking of his glasses. Torvald's sexual attitudes, in a sense, are conditioned by these same spectacles of Hoffmann: a determination to see Nora as an *übermarionette,* a dancing and singing and reciting doll, created for his leisure moments, the maintenance of his household economy, and the convenience of his bed. The myth dies hard, and like so many decaying romantic images, it has a sinister and lingering afterlife, turning up in Hollywood's tales of the Stepford wives and in Alan Ayckbourn's futuristic vision of a suburbia served by doll-helpers in *Henceforward.* Yet the woman's willing capitulation to the social and sexual roles imposed on her by male fantasy perpetuates the myth. Nora has played the game, and in dressing up and dancing once again for Torvald, she suffers by reliving the experience of her role in marriage as another Olympia, just as in the scene with Rank she has clarified and abandoned the meretricious impulses of dollydom that have been raised to painful and embarrassing consciousness. The tarantella is a moment of moral education and spiritual self-discovery for Nora: a painful relinquishment of the doll, the father's plaything, and the husband's toy and the destruction of the secure and macaroon-filled paradise of her doll's house. It is, indeed, a death. But it is also a change to the full and suffering life of a self-reliant, responsible free spirit. Layered deep beneath the romantic myth of the dancing automaton is another, equally compelling theatrical analogue: the miraculous transformation of Aeschylus's chorus of women in *The Eumenides* from precultural chthonic forces into the goddesses of the modern polis, the dancing of the self out of regressive darkness into the light of civilized existence.

THE CHRISTMAS TREE

The most striking visual metonymy of the multiple processes of transformation occurring in the house, however, is the Christmas tree. Nora enters *A Doll's House* blithely happy and humming, laden with gifts for the children, a doll and a doll's cot for the girl, a sword and horse and trumpet for her little boys—gifts that innocuously reveal the stereotypes to which she gives her consent and the extent to which her values are shaped by the social expectations of her world. (She has also surreptitiously smuggled in a packet of macaroons, which she nibbles, like a child among children, only when out of sight of Torvald.) But the grand treat is only momentarily glimpsed, for she instructs the maid to hide away the tree immediately, lest the children see it before it is decorated. The tree is brought onstage again towards the end of act 1, and conspicuously placed in the center of the room as the focal point of Nora's vision of Christmas. By the time the tree is dragged out of concealment, however, Nora's world has already been transformed by the intrusion of a threatening reality in the person of Krogstad. There is something pathetically defensive about her placement of the tree—as if it were a gesture of blatant denial that her Eden is crumbling about her and a desperate attempt to deny that truth by fabricating a sort of talisman against disaster. At one level, the tree functions as a channel of Nora's emotions—not a symbol, but a barometer of feeling. At another level, the tree reveals the woman's psychological strategy of evasion, an attempt to perpetuate an image of family solidarity and happiness against all evidence to the contrary. She transforms the tree fantastically, tinselling and prinking it until it begins to radiate an appalling sense of false and misleading gaiety, becoming an emblem of the deceptive values generated in the dolls' house, ostensibly for the delight of the children. And as she distracts herself with the act of prettifying the tree, so her thoughts turn to the fancy dress ball at the Stenborgs and what she will wear. Masquerade, decoration, dressing up, duplicity—the line between innocuous partying and a damaging denial of reality is difficult to locate, but the tinkering with the tree is clearly emblematic of Nora's assumption of a disguise in a manic attempt to shore up a house on the verge of collapse.

The curtain rises on act 2 to reveal the next stage in the Christmas tree's transformation: it stands tucked away in a corner, "*plukket, forpjusket*" (41), "wrecked and disheveled," with stumps of burnt-out candles, no longer a talismanic protection against the encroachment of external forces on Nora's once secure domain. Again, the tree functions as a conductor of emotional atmosphere. A depressive melancholy has settled over a world bereft of illusions and infects every attempt to resuscitate them with a sense of vanity. The devastated tree now presides over the slow process of self-discovery in which Nora comes to recognize the enemy not as some outside invader of her macaroon-filled paradise, but as the deeply lodged habits of mind and the unconscious responses of a lifetime of dolls' house conditioning. Its transformation into a burnt-out, stripped-down repository of false illusions and evasionary tactics provides a striking visual counterpart to the transformative shocks that will change a doll into a woman through an alteration in moral consciousness.

6

Tragedy without Tears:
Form and Genre

Six preliminary paragraphs precede Ibsen's scenario for an early draft of *A Doll's House,* and it is clear from his subheading, "Notes for the tragedy of modern times," that the finished product is intended to re-shape both the sensibility of the modern mind and the form of modern drama. The new play, evolving from a "drama of modern life" into "*the* tragedy of modern times" ("Commentary," 436; my italics), an-nounces itself as a unique paradox of traditionally incompatible ele-ments: modernity and tragedy, contemporary life and a dramatic form derived from classical antiquity. Can a Norwegian housewife play the tragic hero? Can the dolls' house expand into the realm of the gods? Is the littleness of late nineteenth-century life suitable material for a Sophoclean conflict between woman and her world? What place is there for another Antigone in complacent middle-class life where all tragic gestures are doomed to incomprehension or incredulity? How can the momentous agon of a princess of royal blood battling for her principles against the state in front of the Theban palace "translate" into the terms of a modern world where people no longer do that sort of thing? That ancient heroines belong to ancient times was a truism honored by Ibsen for half his career, during which time he wrote his saga plays about the Viking spirit embodied in the noble women of the historical past, like Lady Inger of Østraat and Hjørdis. Must she now reappear wearing the fancy dress of a Neapolitan fishergirl and dancing a tarantella?

A Doll's House is not the first of Ibsen's modern plays, but it is his first to proclaim tragic intentions. The amalgam of modernity and tragedy in the play represents the emergence of an entirely new genre neither exclusively modern nor tragic, a form of contemporary realism that reaches towards myth, and a tragic structure that traces the heroine's "emancipation by ordeal"[1] without that sense of needless suffering and waste that tragedy demands to set the world aright. With *A Doll's House*, generic descriptions of drama tend to become irrelevant and misleading. Perhaps it is better to call your work a "play unpleasant" and leave it at that, or a "tragedy without tears," or any other of the fanciful iconoclastic forms that Bernard Shaw advised for the post-Ibsen theater with its searing painfulness and its sombre optimism. The technical novelty in Ibsen's "modern tragedy," Shaw argued in *The Quintessence of Ibsenism*, derives from the contemporaneity of *situation*, Ibsen's most significant correction to Shakespeare's outmoded worldview:

> Ibsen saw that . . . the more familiar the situation, the more interesting the play. Shakespear had put ourselves on the stage but not our situations. Our uncles seldom murder our fathers, and cannot legally marry our mothers; we do not meet witches; our kings are not as a rule stabbed and succeeded by their stabbers; and when we raise money by bills we do not promise to pay pounds of our flesh. Ibsen supplies the want left by Shakespear. He gives us not only ourselves, but ourselves in our own situations. The things that happen to his stage figures are things that happen to us. One consequence is that his plays are much more important to us than Shakespear's. Another is that they are capable both of hurting us cruelly and of filling us with excited hopes of escape from idealistic tyrannies, and with visions of intenser life in the future.[2]

Shaw's argument is typically witty in its dismissal of idealism as tyranny and its vision of hopeful evolutionary change. But Shaw misses the complexity and the ambiguity of Ibsen's ending, and Ibsen's endorsement of another type of demanding idealism that galvanizes Nora's slamming of the door on the dolls' house and precipitates the dread that accompanies her escape into a dark, untested freedom.

Exhilaration and catastrophe are inseparable elements in Ibsen's "modern tragedy," and his dénouements leave us—as in the closing moments of *Ghosts*—with the simultaneous sensations of freezing and warmth. But then, so do the final moments of *Oedipus Rex* and *Antony and Cleopatra*. Ibsen's singular achievement is to have shaped his tragedy out of the ordinary raw material of the European middle classes, the scaled down colloquial language of their everyday discourse, and a worldview from which the gods have apparently disappeared.

So much has been written about tragedy, from Aristotle and Boethius through Hegel and Nietzsche and so on to George Steiner and beyond, that I hesitate to engage in further argument and counterargument, in theory countermanded by theory, in the endless debate from which there can be no definitive statement about the essential nature of the tragic vision. I focus on certain elements of tragic form as they relate to the central theme of this analysis—the myth of transformation, the existential reshaping of the self from a composite of socially fashioned roles into an autonomous and free human being on the threshold of redefinition. What is "tragic" about Nora, it seems to me, is precisely what is tragic about Sophocles' Oedipus: both live through a willed and searing deconstruction of a false sense of self—however apparently stable and comfortable, however secure in status and social position—in the will to "reconstruct another being," "*at blevet en anden*" (67), at whatever terrible cost to their well-being. Neither dies, but both experience a painful dying of the old self and an equally painful emergence of a new being, bereft of the certainties and the assumptions that "place" us in a world we think we know. For some, like the chorus in *Oedipus Rex* who speak despairingly of human happiness on this side of the grave, there is little consolation for the suffering of the tragic individual. But Oedipus, who blinds himself against the manifold illusions of a *seeming* world, experiences the elation that comes from freeing himself from false images and semblances, from finding out *who he is* even if that knowledge destroys him. This is the image of the tragic everyman that Yeats projects in "Meru"—the one who rejects the ghosts of his culture and the unquestioned premises that hold civilization together and who actively pursues a career of dangerous inquiry into society, self, and the cosmos:

> but man's life is thought,
> And he, despite his terror, cannot cease
> Ravening through century after century,
> Ravening, raging, and uprooting that he may come
> Into the desolation of reality.[3]

The career of the tragic hero—whether in Sophocles or in Ibsen—seems to move inexorably from Freud's pleasure principle to his reality principle, from the comfortable darkness of happy illusion to the desolation of light and the terror it may reveal. But the heroic temperament is compelled to seek the terror out, to ask question after question even if the answers uproot the stability of the hero's very existence. During the tragic process the hero loses what Ibsen calls *lykke,* a term encompassing all of life's superficial and fleeting happiness, the entire panoply of everyday domestic pleasures that Nora defines in act 1 of *A Doll's House.* The gains are difficult to grasp, even incomprehensible to those who (like Sophocles' chorus and the choral figures in Ibsen) proclaim that one does not do that sort of thing. But to confront reality is to understand oneself, the world in its destructive bent, and the blank indifference of the cosmos to human suffering. The gains are knowledge and an ability to hold desolation in a delicate balance with what Ibsen calls *glæde,* a term encompassing the profound joy of clear-sightedness and insight.

Tragedy questions the unquestionable. It calls traditions of certainty into doubt. It undermines authority and erodes the consolations of faith. It breaks down habitual constructs of intellectual belief and reconstructs deeply disturbing alternatives. In Nora's phrase, it demands *"at komme tilbunds"* (82), "to plumb the depths" of experience, to challenge law and socially regulated duties, to defy even God in the precepts of the church.

The incredulous questions flung at Nora by Torvald when she tells him she is leaving are symptomatic of mankind's desperate clinging to the assurances that define us: "Don't you care what people will say?" "Isn't . . . your duty to your husband and your children?" "Surely you are clear about your position in your own home?" "Haven't you an infallible guide in questions like these?" "Haven't you your religion?" (282). Here are all the notations of human identity, social existence, and psychological security: the functions that define and name us, the unequivocal certainty of our place in the world, the unambiguous value system that enables us to act with confidence, all the reassuring signs that God's in his heaven, all's right with the world. Now, suddenly, Nora finds herself in a strange city without street names, in a country without maps. As a prerequisite for discovering her identity, she must reenvision, recreate everything through an impassioned investigation of the world. For the ultimate tragic question for Nora, as it is for Oedipus, the question at the very heart of the tragic experience, is inevitably a variant on Lear's biting demand: "Who is it that can tell me who I am?" (1.4. 250) At the end of Oedipus's tragic quest for self-identity there is, of course, a biography as fully fashioned as any psychoanalytic restructuring of the shards and fragments of the hidden self. At the end of *A Doll's House*, Nora's emergent selfhood has yet to be defined and the open ending of the play takes her to the brink of desolate reality without a predetermined closure. But, for all their differences in vision, the tragic forms in Sophocles and Ibsen share similarities of patterning that suggest a common source in the rituals and myths of tragic transformation.

Two processes take place simultaneously in *A Doll's House* and *Oedipus Rex*. The first is the protagonists' protracted loss of a sense of self, a disintegration of the being *they thought they were* into an unknown other without the social and domestic connections that defined them. For Nora to find herself a stranger whereas she has formerly been a wife and mother is to *unname* what she has once been, without a nexus of relationships that makes *renaming* possible. What is Oedipus to Jocasta, where once he had been her husband? What is he to Antigone, where once he had been father? And if "husband" and "father" have been the illusions that shape identity and self-definition, what lexicon can name the new reality in which a husband is also a son, and a father is also a brother? In the unreal world of *A Doll's House*, all connections are equally illusory: "wife" and "mother" are merely semblances, variants on a mechanical game of happy families wherein dolls masquerade as human beings.

Tragedy, in its essence, is the experience of this ripping apart. The phase of the tragic mythos that the Greeks called *sparagmos* is an experience of distintegration, chaos, and collapse. For Nora deconstructing the doll's role means finding, as when Peer Gynt strips the layers of his onion, a blank nothingness at the core of life. In *Oedipus* this experience takes the form of a relentless questioning of identity that snaps every link that binds man to his family, undermines the confidence that sanctions self-assertion, and finally reduces his entire existence to a charade of false assumptions. But even as he loses his identity as Polybos's beloved son, so the awful reality of Laios's parricide reshapes Oedipus's sense of self—the self one sees in nightmares, perhaps, but a self that restructures reality and reintegrates the disintegrating personality. For every loss he suffers, an awesome substitution takes its place. For every false illusion he forfeits, a desolate truth redefines the man he really is. And so he presses on, demanding self-knowledge in the face of mounting terror—"How could I wish that I were someone else? / How could I not be glad to know my birth?"[4]—until the "someone else" is finally discarded as the not-self and the authentic Oedipus stands recreated as the self that terrifies and gladdens. This process of reintegration that accompanies the dying "someone else" is what the Greeks call *anagnorisis*: the counterexperience of recovery, self-ordering, and restoration. The process is often cheerless in the desolate reality it uncovers, but despite all the terror the heroic temperament will rage toward this confrontation.

For Oedipus, the reconstruction of the self is as appalling as its deconstruction, and his recognition of that new self is as painful as the dying of his inauthentic self. For Nora, the tragedy is without tears if only because the resurrecting self looks forward to a new woman fashioned out of her own recovered moral sensibility. And Ibsen's "modern tragedy" defies the gods and their unalterable sway, denies all systems that predetermine the course of human destiny, and refuses to acknowledge that Apollo, god of clarity, light, and knowledge, reveals a merely unendurable reality. If Nora's *anagnorisis* is simultaneous with the *sparagmos* of the doll-wife and mother, then the self-respecting woman she becomes through trial and error and difficult experience will mitigate the ordeal of her fearful emancipation. The rhythm of the play is composed of a plot structure that, blow by blow, deprives the doll of her complacency and isolates her from every source of comfort and support, but impels her—at moments of moral crisis—to dredge authentic selfhood out of a lifetime of social conditioning and fashion a new and untested identity out of the fragments of a shattered life.

The stages of deprivation and isolation are stark and episodic in an almost Sophoclean structure. John Northam, in "Ibsen's Search for the Hero," has offered an excellent sequential account of the play's plot lines and the emergence of Nora as a modern tragic heroine, and I feel at liberty, therefore, to deal with the key incidents in *A Doll's House* in a discontinuous analysis spread throughout the chapters of this study. But the spine of Nora's tragic experience, *anagnorisis* deriving from *sparagmos,* must be grasped as the central, unifying vision of the play. The process of ever deepening despair brings her face to face with death, even as it reveals the moral courage that enables her to endure the loss of all of life's happiness. Like Oedipus's predicament, hers is clarified in a series of interviews and confrontations wherein, in flashes of visionary insight, a deeply suppressed self-knowledge suddenly erupts into consciousness and realigns the contents of her intellectual and moral life. What is most extraordinary about these moments is the lived through experience of thought in the process of being formulated, of existence in the process of being changed. Nora constantly surprises the audience because she constantly surprises herself—not in a steadily unfolding revelation of consciousness but in the momentary epiphanies of the woman aghast, every now and then, at the doll within. For "doll" and "not-doll" occupy equal dimensions in the psychic life, and the fascination of the role lies in the double nature of a character who is simultaneously a macaroon-nibbling child-wife and a heroine of the ethical life. It is the prerogative of the actress playing Nora to discover those epiphanies that enable her, fragment by fragment, to dismantle the doll and reconstitute the woman out of the subconscious revelations of authentic selfhood.

Little by little the doll dies, and the walls of the dolls' house begin to crack. As director, I would ask the actress playing Nora to discover those moments as early in the action as possible. In the first "interview" with Mrs. Linde, for instance, the self-demeaning strategies of dollydom and its fearful insecurities are laid momentarily bare and Nora sees, frighteningly, a truth that she cannot bear to face. More obviously, a breakdown occurs in the Krogstad "interviews" when the doll's house world is dangerously invaded and Nora is stripped of every defense against ruin and despair—every defense, that is to say, except the most available: denial, disavowal of the unprovable facts, and dishonesty. Because she will not demean herself by lying about an action motivated by love and compassion, she commits herself to the consequences of destroying the dolls' house. The doll has an easy way out, but there is no easy way out for the woman. Better death than cheap humiliation. With her back to the wall, Nora tries one final ploy: she tries to wheedle money from Dr. Rank in the habitual mode of the sexually titillating doll, until in self-dismay she abandons both the disgusting dolly strategy and the last opportunity of extricating herself from a desperate predicament. Isolated from every hope, deprived of all illusions, terrified of incriminating her husband in her crime and corrupting her children with the squalor of inherited depravity, Nora commits herself to the inevitability of death. "People don't do that sort of thing" (254), Krogstad reminds her. But in a no-exit situation, there seems to be no alternative. In an ecstasy of despair, she dances a *totentanz*, which whirls her into the very epicenter of her *sparagmos*—an agony of destruction in which the dying Neapolitan doll abandons herself to chaos and despair and out of which the woman emerges in a miraculous *anagnorisis* of recovered fortitude and stoical resolve.

One last illusion remains, one vestige of the doll's mentality that assuages her pain and reconfirms the values of her shattered house—the belief that, when the world falls apart, Torvald will remain a pillar of altruistic self-sacrifice and prove himself a man worth dying for. But Torvald falls apart in the last 15 minutes of the play, and the shattering of the male-doll is more terrible than anything that Nora had consciously anticipated, finally confirming woman's necessary independence from a world of fantasy and false romantic expectation. Perhaps in "tragedy without tears" people no longer do "that sort of thing," but if they do not kill themselves, it is not for lack of will or courage. To endure, to live in a world without signs or codes or certainties is painful enough. It is the tragedy of modern times.

THE NEW DRAMATIC FORMS

A Doll's House, as I have suggested, presents an ancient structure in a new dramatic form and, in so doing, reinterprets tragedy for the modern world. The new form is compounded of two "isms" and a third generic mode: naturalism, realism, and the *pièce bien faite* (well-made play) or the *drame à thèse* (problem play), which were staples of the boulevard theaters of nineteenth-century Europe. Like "tragedy," these terms are variously defined and difficult to extricate from one another, but each has its own theoretical premises. To grasp their ideologies is to understand how the *Doll's House* revolution both draws upon and devastates traditional and inherited forms of theater. For if theater is indeed a mirror held up to nature, a reflecting surface in which society sees the times depicted, then theater has the power to shape that image and challenge the audience to respond. But if theater endorses the comfortable and habitual view of man and his world, it merely perpetuates those ghost-ridden systems and opposes itself to dynamic social change. Shaw consistently attacked this sort of dead theater, taking his cue from Ibsen, the "hero of the new departure" who finally persuaded Europe to take its conscience and brains with it to the theater. "I fight the theatre," Shaw wrote in this preface to one of his most unpleasant plays, "not with pamphlets and sermons and treatises, but with plays."[5] His battle was waged as hotly against old dead ideas and morbid beliefs as against the very forms that enshrined them, and the first effective blow struck by the avant-garde against the unreflecting habits and the stale forms of the boulevard theaters, Shaw argued, was *A Doll's House*.

Paradoxically, *A Doll's House* so closely resembles the material it attacks that an audience might easily be beguiled into a sense of false security and anticipate the traditional resolution of a sort of late nineteenth-century soap opera. Its heroine (if she could afford to) would probably have spent her free evenings at the theater, immersed in what Shaw called "Sardoodledom," the repertoire of Sardou and Scribe and their Danish imitators who could be relied upon to endorse all the sentimental romantic clichés of contemporary social thought. Nora's every assumption is shaped by the values of popular culture, and her fantasies are conditioned by the basic dramatic premises of the well-made play, a term, as Stephen Stanton suggests in his anthology of typical examples,[6] that has become synonymous with trashy playwriting. And the television sitcom has proved that the value system enshrined in the well-made play has been immune to the advent of Ibsen and Shaw. "You go to the theatre for relaxation and amusement," said Scribe, "not for instruction or correction. Now what most amuses you is not truth but fiction. . . . The theatre is therefore rarely the direct expression of social life . . . it is often the inverse expression."[7]

The essentially *fictional* and *inverted expression* of social existence is precisely what the Helmers cling to against all evidence to the contrary—even, in the final confrontation, in which they enact their own little well-made scenarios in a farcical breakdown of Scribean theatrical convention. In the Scribean view of life, dramatic art no longer holds the mirror up to nature, instead it touches up reality, like a photographer carefully removing the warts and blemishes from the negative so that the image corresponds to what his client would *prefer* to see. (Ibsen's Hjalmar Ekdal in *The Wild Duck* is precisely such a photographic inverter of life's crude realities.) And, in keeping with its artificial view of experience, the well-made play demands a highly artificial construction even more straitjacketing than the conventions of the rule-bound classical theater.

As a social problem or *drame à thèse,* Scribe's sort of play presents issues that demand an easy resolution without disturbing the moral code of the middle-class audience or its preference for sentimental reconciliations. The vast outpouring of rewritten and edited versions of *A Doll's House* by those appalled at Ibsen's betrayal of Scribe and Sardou provides depressing examples of the sort of sitcom dénouements that the average theatergoer would have clearly preferred. The first version of *A Doll's House* to appear on the English stage was a piece of pure Sardoodledom by Henry Arthur Jones and Henry Herman entitled *Breaking a Butterfly* (1884), a play that enacts the fantasy life of Ibsen's Helmers in a series of multiple inversions of reality. "Burlesque," wrote Granville-Barker, "could do no more": "Torvald-Humphrey behaves like the paste-board hero of Nora's doll's house dream; he *does* strike his chest and say 'I am the guilty one.' And Nora-Flora cries that she is a poor weak foolish girl, '. . . no wife for a man like you. You are a thousand times too good for me,' and never wakes up and walks out of her doll's house at all."[8] Nora's behavior is, indeed, predicated on this sort of Scribean assumption, just as Torvald's fantasy ending is perfectly replicated in one of the excruciating German "fourth act" additions. In the German version of the play, Torvald returns home bearing a family-sized box of macaroons for a contrite Nora (whose current condition is hinted at in tiny garments crafted by Mrs. Linde). "Have you really and truly forgiven me?" she asks, and Torvald responds by lovingly popping a macaroon in her mouth. "The miracle of miracles!" cries Nora chewing happily ("Commentary," 457). Ironically, this is precisely the sort of scenario that both Nora and Torvald try to force on events at the end of the original play, and which Ibsen resists to the bitter end.

All the well-made features of what Torvald calls the "*komedies-pil*" (77)—Nora's "playacting"—cunningly entrap an unwary audience into accepting the extraordinary as the conventional. Indeed, as Shaw points out, "up to a certain point in the last act, A Doll's House is a play that might be turned into a very ordinary French drama by the excision of a few lines, and the substitution of a sentimental happy ending for the famous last scene."[9] Most of the structural features that make up the commercially successful formula popularized by Scribe, and later petrified into "rules" by manuals like William Archer's *Playmaking* (1928), appear in *A Doll's House*: the plot driven by a deep dark secret, suspensefully revealed through expository interviews, documents, letters, or a variety of coincidental accidents; the fluctuation of the heroine's fortunes leading to the critical *scène à faire*, or "obligatory" climax of the action; then the peripeteia, or disastrous reversal of expectations, occasioned by the revelation of damaging information about her past; a fundamental misunderstanding, the quid pro quo, which delays the satisfactory resolution of personal problems; and, finally, a dénouement that negates all difficulties, cuts through the tangled web of complications and restores the status quo by reasserting the standard moral position.[10]

Using Scribean conventions against Scribean intentions, Ibsen gives his audience what it had come to expect in its inattentive moments, and then, in the last 15 minutes, he suddenly wrenches the structure of the *pièce bien faite* into a strange new configuration. "Formerly," writes Shaw, "you had in what was called a well-made play an exposition in the first act, a situation in the second, and unravelling in the third. Now you have exposition, situation, and discussion; and discussion is the test of the playwright. . . . It was by this new technical feature: this addition of a new movement, as musicians would say, to the dramatic form, that *A Doll's House* conquered Europe and founded a new school of dramatic art."[11] Shaw was jubilant. Ibsen had made it impossible, now, to pass off mere spite against unconventional conduct as morality, or idle twaddling as comment on the serious problems of life, or the hypocritial lies of the well-made tradition as forms of vital truth. Instead of a theater of stage magicians' tricks, *A Doll's House*, according to Shaw, is a truly representative theater

in which a domestic story which is word for word the true story of half our households, first deepens to tragedy, and then sublimates and vanishes, leaving its two figures no longer the Helmer and Nora of the story, but the types of Man and Woman at the point where they now stand, she revealing the new Will in her before which must yield all institutions hostile to it—his harem, his nursery, his lust and superstition, in their established forms of home duties, family ties, and chivalry: he dimly beginning to see that in giving this irresistible Will its way he is not losing her, since he never really possessed her, but standing at last to win her for the first time.[12]

The innovative form that Ibsen introduced to the European theater is "tragedy without tears," salvaged from the flood of tears without tragedy with which Scribe and Sardou and Henry Arthur Jones and Henry Herman and several decades of hackwork had inundated the stages of the nineteenth century.

THE MELODRAMA

The disruption of the expected Scribean resolution made nonsense of yet another dramatic mode—the melodrama, with its crude division of people and ideas into the unequivocally "right" and "wrong." Instead of a black-and-white conflict, the drama now arises (as Shaw noted) as a conflict of unsettled ideals, that is to say, by means of a genuinely dialectical argument between two creditable positions, each driven by a set of imperatives that makes it difficult for absolute truth to settle comfortably on one side or the other. There is no unqualified "right," no dismissible "wrong" in the new drama, but there is a genuine difference of vision and an extraordinary capacity for one extreme to accommodate the limited truth of the other. The Ibsenian *tvertimod*—the frame of mind that enables Ibsen to contemplate two contradictory views simultaneously—ensures a continuing debate, a constantly shifting point of truth in the spectrum of human possibilities, and an open-ended form that leaves issues unresolved after the curtain falls.

Melodrama leaves no room for divergent opinion or for the complexity of human temperament. Its single vision demands closure, certain resolution, and consistency, and its character types are drawn to scale. An audience habituated to easy moral distinctions might be inclined to see Krogstad as the stock villain of melodrama—the dastardly blackmailer intent on bringing the heroine to ruination. Instead, Ibsen emphasizes the social forces that motivate Krogstad's "villainy," and in the place of endemic evil Ibsen reveals a human being capable of momentous moral change.

Part of Nora's difficulty is that she succumbs too readily to the melodramatic frame of mind, not only in her evaluation of people but in her code of conduct. For if Nora's value system has been shaped by the cultural philosophy of the *pièce bien faite*, her behavior betrays many of the technical features of melodramatic theater—the broad gestural emoting, the scaled-down telegrammatic style of her utterance, the self-dramatizing heroics, the fantasy of suicide. Ibsen's conscious intention of fighting the contemporary theater with plays is nowhere more apparent than in the metatheatrical touches that structure *A Doll's House*: the "*komediespil*" (playacting) that his characters script for themselves and act out is a counterpoint to the tragedy in which he envelops them. Nora's melodramatic scenario permeates the play at every level, culminating in a crescendo of exaggerated stage business at the climax of *her* encapsulated drama:

> NORA: (*gropes around her, wild-eyed, seizes Helmer's cloak, wraps it round herself, and whispers quickly, hoarsely, spasmodically.*) Never see him again. Never, never, never. And never see the children again either. Never, never. (275)

And so the "*komediespil*" proceeds until Torvald draws Nora's attention to the theatricality of her responses, which are grotesquely inappropriate in the circumstances. But Nora is also farcical in her plagiarizing (consciously or not) of the mechanized emotions of melodrama. She steps, at this crucial moment of realization, out of the inauthentic world of late nineteenth-century theater into the new realism, out of the conditioned gestural acting of the stage doll into the vitality of the new "*gjennemlevende*," or "lived through" style of the transformed woman, out of Scribe and into Ibsen.

In one sense, Ibsen thoroughly subverts the dramatic genres he incorporates into his plays. In another sense, he exploits them in technically innovative ways. The tarantella—a diverting musical dance number that intensifies the emotional moment, supplements the action, and displaces language with spectacle—leaps straight out of the melodramatic entr'acte. In *A Doll's House* the tarantella satisfies all of the expectations of the dramatic genres in the very act of transcending them. The dance becomes, as I have already suggested in a previous chapter, a visual metaphor of Nora's unspeakable experience, a symbolic dance of death in which the doll self perishes, and a mythic act of transformation through which the new woman emerges. Melodrama's simple physical spectacle suddenly becomes a complex spiritual epiphany, yet the *reality* of the moment or the continuity of the action is not violated. A woman rehearses a dance in her living room, and the normative becomes our entrée into the deep recesses of the soul life. Ibsen's innovative style absorbs the melodrama and the *pièce bien faite* even as it rejects their value systems and the hackneyed conventions that delimit their vision.

REALISM

The great challenge that *A Doll's House* poses to reader, director, and actress is the difficulty of negotiating a path through the simultaneous theatrical genres—a Sophoclean tragic structure, ironically rooted in the conventions of the *pièce bien faite,* sporadically punctuated with episodes from Nora's melodramatic scenario, and all subsumed into what Shaw called the "new theatre" of Ibsen's realism.

The *modernity* in "the tragedy of modern times" derives, in large measure, from its style: it is nondirective where the *pièce bien faite* had been didactic; it is normative where traditional tragedy had dealt with the exceptional; and it is universal where the melodrama had been concerned with very specific solutions to social ills. Instead of preaching a sermon, realism challenges the audience to see the complexity of reality, the contradictory wholeness within the dialectics of experience, but without the appearance of authorial selection or moral suasion. "In none of my plays," wrote Ibsen of *Ghosts,* "is the author so extrinsic, so completely absent, as in this last one" (476). This statement succinctly summarizes the realist creed and carefully dissociates it from the self-dramatizing style of the romantics and the self-analytical style of the later expressionists. Dogmatism is shelved in the interests of truth, and a dispassionate observation (as through the eye of a camera) ensures a view of the world untrammeled by personal opacity or social myopia.

In *A Doll's House* one senses a decisive shift in tragic style from the antiquarian re-creation of an unverifiable past to the normative values of the everyday, from *Catiline* and *The Vikings at Helgeland* to the tragedy of the lady next door. It is no longer the aristocratic exemplar of greatness who models man's tragic experience but the unexceptional and the everyday. After *A Doll's House* we are challenged to seek out heroic magnitude in ordinary and day-to-day existence and recognize the universality of Nora's experience.[13] This aim is the basic theoretical injunction that Émile Zola imposed on the new school of realism: "*Faire vraie*"—"represent reality *truthfully,*" capture its immediacy, and make its concerns vitally contemporaneous. For the only verifiable truth we can know is the world of scientifically observable phenomena, and there must be no historical distance between the heroine's experience and the spectator's, and nothing should dissociate an audience from the tragedy of modern times.

Nothing, however, could be more ephemeral than the sort of "relevance" implicit in Zola's theories, for realism, as a theatre of immediacy, constantly runs the risk of receding into the mummified time of museum drama. Ibsen must surely have been aware of the fallacies of Zola's injunction to "be truthful" and the danger of falling out of the frying pan of antiquarian realism into the fire of slice-of-life realism with its narrow specificities, its photographic surfaces, and instantly exhaustible issues.

The great achievement of *A Doll's House* is making the hard and static world of phenomenal reality the vehicle of myth, just as it converts the unemphatic and strictly functional language of colloquial speech into a resonant form of prose-poetry that honors Zola's principle of "simplicity" without sinking into banality. "*Faire simple*": create a drama of maximal sufficiency to which nothing can be added and nothing removed without radically affecting the structure, and find significant utterance not in blank verse or Alexandrines but in the far more difficult art of prose. Above all, make *truth* and *simplicity* synonymous with the momentous and timeless issues. For this is Zola's final injunction to the realist school of drama: "*Faire grand*"—reveal the "bigness" of life, the complexity of reality, the disturbingly unresolvable dialectics of experience. This is the theory implicit in Ibsen's revolutionary "tragedy of modern times."

One other "-ism" must be accounted for: naturalism, the secular vision of a scientific age that transformed fate, chance, and the gods into current theories of heredity and environment and, in Shaw's phrase, caused the "banishment of conscience from human affairs . . . [and] mind from the universe."[14] This determinist frame of mind that imprisons creation in genetic inheritance, physical location, and biological process is shared by nearly every character in Ibsen's play. Torvald believes that inherited characteristics condition one's moral nature and pollute one's environment. Rank suffers congenitally from the sins of his father and regards the whole world as a moral leper colony. For Krogstad, man is the base product of a society that shapes his very existence. Nora unthinkingly accepts the vision of women as ineluctably controlled by puppet masters in the dolls' house world she is fated to inhabit. Crushed between the millstones of "race" and "milieu," between her father's transmission of moral degeneracy and her place in an inflexible male-dominated social structure that dooms her to proscribed forms of behavior, Nora at first accepts her status in the house as a naturalistic doll without volition, without control over her existence, and without the freedom to change.

Banishing mind from the universe means accepting one's fate as a given, abdicating moral responsibility, and embracing helplessness in the face of a universe that predetermines life and place and social destiny. The doll's house is pervaded by this spirit of hopelessness. It is a milieu of fixed categories, a naturalist emblem in which environmental fate is given the dignity of godhead, and a paradigm of the inescapable condition of human existence. When Nora finally slams the door of this house, she also slams the door on the banished conscience and the determinist philosophy tht would cripple her will and subjugate it to forces beyond her control. Her destiny, unlike Oedipus's, is avoidable. Change, moral transformation, and an intellectual reordering of her thinking all lie within her control. For Ibsen, the tragedy of modern times is the existentialist's tragedy for whom no God is unquestionable, no dogma absolutely unassailable, no abstraction beyond challenge. Woman ceases to function as a mere organism, gradually accommodating herself through evolutionary process to the milieu best suited to her social function. In finally wrenching herself free, Nora restores conscience to the universe, autonomy to the human spirit, and hope to those who fear the desolation of reality.

7

Nora's Mirror Images:
Anne Marie, Krogstad, Rank

In *Hamlet* three young men share a similar condition: each has lost a father and responds to the death in his own particular manner. Laertes and Fortinbras provide a vital system of reflecting mirrors in which Hamlet finds a perspective for his own predicament and against which he defines his mode of coping with a universal theme.

Parallelism and juxtaposition are fundamental principles in dramatic structure and techniques in which the mere presence of another onstage character reveals the inner life of the protagonist with economy and complexity. Because Ibsen's realistic style denies his characters the introspective and revelatory nature of Shakespearean soliloquy, the mirror device must serve even more vitally to incorporate every character in a series of kaleidoscopic reflections. There are no small parts in these plays (as Stanislavski, in another context, admonished his actors), and even those who appear only for a few minutes in a scene or two become mirrors in which Nora finds her destiny reflected. The old nursemaid, Anne Marie, is a case in point.

ANNE MARIE

An important fixture in the dolls' house world, Anne Marie is a surrogate mother not only for Nora's children, but for Nora herself. "My poor little Nora never had any other mother but me" (236), she reminds Nora, vaguely suggesting the half-orphaned state of the child brought up in a father-dominated home and cared for by a doting nanny who had been deprived of her own illegitimate daughter. To Anne Marie, Nora is still "*lille Nora, stakker*" (42); "little Nora, poor wee creature." She fusses over Nora, fearful of her catching cold in the dreadful weather, and generally treats her as a child among her children. Anne Marie is the loving, uncritical heart of the nursery world whose few scenes are infused with the traditional platitudes of the nanny and the uncritical and unthinking viewpoint of the working-class nineteenth-century serving woman who accepts her social position as her destiny.

For Nora, Anne Marie is the mirror of the woman deprived of her children, the test case for her own necessary relinquishment of her babies to the kindness of strangers:

> NORA: Do you think they would forget their Mummy if she went away for good?
>
> NURSEMAID: Good gracious—for good?
>
> NORA: Tell me, Anne Marie—I've often wondered—how on earth could you bear to hand your child over to strangers?
>
> NURSEMAID: Well, there was nothing else for it when I had to come and nurse my little Nora.
>
> NORA: Yes but . . . how could you *bring* yourself to do it?
>
> NURSEMAID: When I had the chance of such a good place? When a poor girl's been in trouble she must make the best of things. Because *he* didn't help, the rotter.
>
> NORA: But your daughter will have forgotten you.
>
> NURSEMAID: Oh no, she hasn't. She wrote to me when she got confirmed, and again when she got married. (236)

Anne Marie's is a pathetic account of a devastated life, all the more so for the understated, compliant tone in which the woman accepts the conditions imposed on her by social morality, the class structure, and economics. Without rights to child support, without alimony, and without protection she acquiesces in what seems to her inevitable. The loss of her child is simply something she must bear. And just as children "get used to anything in time," as she points out (236), so her estrangement from her daughter recedes into the habitual and the commonplace. Two letters in a lifetime are as much as she expects.

Nora, of course, expects nothing. She intends to die, not relinquish her children, and she needs to be reassured that the loving heart will care for them as she had once cared for her little Nora. In a sense, Nora's estrangement has already begun. Accepting without question Torvald's theories of the maternal corruption of children through lies and deceit, Nora has already begun to withdraw from the pleasure of being with her babies, leaving them for longer periods of time with Anne Marie. Like the pathetically limited servant, she accepts unquestioningly the unwritten law that makes her unfit to bring up her children. In the final moments of the play she dismisses the ridiculous theory of moral infection and comes to understand the crucial failure of her parenting: she has been playing doll-mother with doll-babies, keeping them in ignorance of the world, and perpetuating the sex-based stereotypes of the dolls' house even in her choice of Christmas gifts. The scene in act 1 in which she romps with the children in a game of hide-and-seek is as indispensable to Ibsen's image of the loving mother as it is to our understanding of her infantilism: she delights in them as "*mit søde lille dukkebarn*" (29), "*små dejlike dukkebørn*" (29); her "sweet and pretty little baby dollies." Her tragedy is that in relinquishing her "*dukkebørn*," as she believes she must, she also leaves behind three very real children who will in time probably get used to her absence, may indeed forget her.

Nora's leaving the children was the single most controversial aspect of *A Doll's House* for Ibsen's contemporaries. Clement Scott, critic of the *Theatre* in 1889, was typically vehement in his condemnation. Nora, he claimed, committed an unnatural offense unworthy of even the lower animals: "A cat or dog would tear anyone who separated it from its offspring, but the socialistic Nora, the apostle of the new creed of humanity, leaves her children without a pang."[1] Hedwig Niemann-Raabe, the German actress cast to play Nora, refused to enact what she considered an outrage to her own domestic values and demanded an alternative ending, which Ibsen, cursing the "barbaric outrage" he was forced to commit against his play, eventually provided. In that version, Torvald drags Nora to the door of the children's bedroom and forces her to look at her sweetly sleeping children who are innocent of their potentially motherless fate and reminds her of her own half-orphaned childhood. This experience is too much for Nora and she succumbs.

> NORA: Motherless! (*Struggles with herself, lets her travelling bag fall, and says.*) Oh, this is a sin against myself, but I cannot leave them. (*Half sinks down by the door.*) (288)

This is a dénouement worthy of Scribe, except for the phrase about committing a sin against herself, which, once again, calls into question the coping strategies of Anne Marie and Nora's original intention to abandon her children by committing suicide.

Anne Marie's "sin" has been her passive acceptance of the treatment meted out by an indifferent man, coupled with her confusion of alterable circumstances with ineluctable fate. "Getting used to things" and "making the best of things" and succumbing to a "nothing else for it" philosophy sums up the terms of her fatalism: "*Det måtte jeg jo*" (42); "it had to be like that for me." The Nora who slams the door on the dolls' house may be subject to the same economic deprivations, but she is not subject to the cultural compulsions that have conditioned Anne Marie's deterministic vision. To "sin" against herself in this way may be a more heinous "sin" against her children than leaving them to the care of strangers. Ibsen implies as much in a speculative comment on the Noras and Mrs. Alvings of the late Victorian world: "These women of the modern age, mistreated as daughters, as sisters, as wives, not educated in accordance with their talents, debarred from following their mission, deprived of their inheritance, embittered in mind—these are the ones who supply the mothers for the new generation. What will be the result?" ("Commentary," 468). The sin Ibsen describes may be worse than the "sin" for which Clement Scott castigates the absconding feminist/socialist who trades unselfishness for self-sufficiency and thereby violates a fundamental law of nature. But, again, there is a substantial difference between the Nora whose deep misgivings about her parenting persuade her to *educate* herself for the responsibility and the Nora whose dream of suicide subordinates the well-being of her children to her own romantic yearning. It is perverse to maintain, with Clement Scott, that Nora "forgets . . . her very instinct as a mother, forgets the three innocent children who are asleep in the next room, forgets her responsibilities, and does a thing that one of the lower animals would not do" (Egan, 114). Nora's acute *mindfulness* of these very factors possesses her, converts her conscious decision into a tragic necessity, and intensifies her painful metamorphosis from doll-mother into woman. It is rather Anne Marie who has forgotten her child, who has left it without a pang, and whose motives for child abandonment bring into focus the vastly different set of motivations that impel Nora to question her adequacy as a doll-mother for the new generation.

KROGSTAD

Krogstad is a mirror that throws back at Nora the reflection of a persecuted criminal in an unforgiving society, the image of the victim whose fatal error has been accommodating a system that destroys him. One of the great surprises of the play, says Shaw, is that Torvald, *not* Krogstad, turns out to be the true villain of the piece. This is a neat inversion of melodramatic expectations, if, indeed, melodramatic conventions are relevant to the vision of *A Doll's House*. The apparent "heavy," Krogstad is a strange mixture of frailties, a man simultaneously pathetic and repellent who serves as a catalyst for unleashing the censure of small-minded and uncharitable provincial moralists. He belongs to the mercantile set of civil servants, lawyers, and bank officials, and his unforgivable crime has been to offend—for whatever reason—the superstringency of their ethical codes. This is how society treats its moral lepers. And this is how it will ostracize Nora if her crime is ever revealed, for Krogstad and Nora are fellow criminals beneath the skin.

Krogstad has come to see Nora not primarily to threaten but to plead as a suppliant for his jeopardized position in the bank, to impress his pathetic humanity on her and persuade her to use her boasted influence over her husband in his favor. Nora assumes a hostile, supercilious attitude to this subordinate whose career is at her pleasure, but when pressed to exercise her power in the dolls' house, she admits quite candidly that she has none. An incredulous Krogstad explains his predicament more fully: retaining his position is not a matter of money but of social rehabilitation and respectability. He has spent years establishing himself once again after his "trouble," and the bank clerk's position will enable him to give up loan-sharking and support his sons in an honorable fashion. Torvald is about to kick him back into the mud, and Krogstad is now engaged in a desperate struggle for his life.

Nora's response to his implied threat of disclosure is ugly and defensive. She condemns his behavior as shameful, brutal, and nasty— the actions of "*hvilket slet menneske*" (32); "a thoroughly vile human being." And he retaliates by making her look in the mirror. Point by point, he establishes their criminal affinity. Corroborative details fall rapidly into place: the note for the debt was dated three days after Nora's father died, and the handwriting of the date didn't match the father's signature. But the evidence of forgery is tenuous in the extreme, and the discrepancies can be convincingly explained away. Krogstad is an intelligent lawyer and knows that he cannot really pin a case to the documentary evidence, so he asks a point-blank question and elicits a stunning response:

KROGSTAD: What really matters is the signature. And *that* is of course genuine, Mrs. Helmer? It really was your father who wrote his name here?

> NORA: (*after a moment's silence, throws her head back and looks at him defiantly.*) No, it wasn't. It was me who signed father's name. (228)

Here is one of those extraordinary quantum leaps in Nora's emergent moral sensibility: she commits herself to death and torment rather than taking the easy way out by lying and subterfuge—"*ved kneb og kunstgreb*" (38); "with trickery and guile" (as Torvald describes Krogstad's strategy in identical circumstances). She is offered the opportunity to wriggle out, and in a courageous acceptance of consequence she refuses to demean herself any further. The Viking temperament within the suburban housewife will not allow her to be humiliated by those who already scorn her. Hedda Gabler, trapped and driven to the wall by Brack, shows the same defiant refusal to diminish herself "*ved kneb og kunstgreb*." "Better death," Hedda tells him, and this becomes the unspoken resolve beneath all of Nora's subsequent decisions.

Krogstad insists on a parallelism of mirror images at the very point when Nora's differences are becoming most apparent. They have committed the same criminal act, and perhaps (although Nora incredulously questions it) for the self same motives:

> KROGSTAD: Mrs. Helmer, it's quite clear you still haven't the faintest idea what it is you've committed. But let me tell you, my own offence was no more and no worse than that, and it ruined my entire reputation.
>
> NORA: You? Are you trying to tell me that you once risked everything to save your wife's life?
>
> KROGSTAD: The law takes no account of motives.
>
> NORA: Then they must be very bad laws.
>
> KROGSTAD: Bad or not, if I produce this document in court, you'll be condemned according to them.
>
> NORA: I don't believe it. Isn't a daughter entitled to try and save her father from worry and anxiety on his deathbed? Isn't a wife entitled to save her husband's life? I might not know very much about the law, but I feel sure of one

thing: it must say somewhere that things like this are
allowed. (229)

Legality and justice, business value and humane value—"*forretninger*"
and "*bevæggrunde*" (35)—no longer coincide in mankind's experience, if they ever did. The morality of the state, as Antigone had already discovered nearly 2,500 years before *A Doll's House*, is by no
means synonymous with the natural justice of the loving heart, and
although an individual sense of moral decency may insist on the pri-
macy of motive in judging human actions, the law makes no conces-
sion to specific circumstance.

Krogstad has fallen victim to this cruel discrepancy in social morality, but instead of rejecting its operation he has found a way of
exploiting it to his advantage. Armed with the law of business trans-
action, he persecutes as he has been persecuted, supporting the operation of a machine that has already engulfed him. At this point the
mirror begins to reveal a set of obverse images. Krogstad battles
against the system by deploying it against society, whereas Nora subverts that system by postulating a radical alternative that cannot co-
exist with the law of the state, except in some third empire of the ideal
political life. Her mode of thought, like that of Antigone, is a danger
to the state, a form of lateral thinking that challenges tradition and
calls into question the wisdom of a male-dominated morality that does
not take women's perspectives into account. "There are two kinds of
moral law," Ibsen wrote in his notes for the play, "two kinds of conscience, one in man and a completely different one in woman" ("Commentary," 436): *her* "natural instinct" claims equality with *his*
"authority," *her* trust in love displaces *his* trust in legality as a moti-
vating force in human affairs. "I did it for love, didn't I?" (229), Nora
cries. Her ethical sensibility, like Antigone's, is prelegal, premoral; it
equates *right* with *natural impulse*. Nora's great subversive challenge
to the man's world is the genuinely revolutionary impulse at the heart
of the play.

In pleading Krogstad's case before Torvald, Nora is, of course,
pleading her own, and she, like Antigone, is testing the capacity of

Creon to acknowledge the Antigone principle. Can Krogstad be condemned as wicked, she inquires, if he acted out of *need*? But "*nød*" (38)—"dire necessity" or "destitution"—belongs to the womanly realm of motive, and Torvald ignores Nora's argument for mercy in favor of man's unrelenting social judgment. In Torvald's view Krogstad acted, like so many other delinquents, "*i ubesindighed*" (38)—"senselessly and foolishly". Those who act as Krogstad did are moral lepers, the outcasts of society, polluters of their family who hide corruption from their children beneath the mask of respectability and infect the very air the children breathe. Unless they expiate their guilt through punishment, he finally maintains, such sinners will continue to make Torvald feel nauseous.

These, then, are the poles of Ibsen's dialectics: law of the state and law of the heart; social conscience and individual conscience, legality and human instinct. "The wife in the play," writes Ibsen, "ends up quite bewildered and not knowing right from wrong; her natural instincts on the one side and her faith in authority on the other leave her completely confused" ("Commentary," 436). Her confusion, moreover, is magnified and distorted in the "mirror" as she transfers to her own parallel situation Torvald's moral opprobrium, his denunciation of the corrupting parent, his demand for punishment, and his physical revulsion from Krogstad's case. She cannot credit Torvald's moralistic theory with the truth, nor can she exonerate herself from his judgment. The loathing and the fear she feels for Krogstad gradually begin to taint her sense of self and edge her toward a self-inflicted death beneath the ice.

In her second interview with Krogstad, the two pathetic outcasts discuss suicide and the courage it takes to go through with it. His motives for seeing her are, as usual, a curious mixture of self-seeking advantage and gruff concern for a companion in misery. He asks her, in turn, to regard him as a human being, not merely as a functionary in the economic world but as a man with some residual "*hjertelag*" (57); "the kindness of heart" that prompts him to sympathize with a woman pushed to the end of her endurance. What frightens him about his fight for life is the thought of the casualty it might claim in innocent human life, and his aggressive tactics exist in uneasy alliance with his sympathy for one who has suffered a similar trauma. Suicide, as he knows, is a solution for the desperate, but it takes tremendous courage. He is relieved to find in Nora a kindred spirit in cowardice, one who lacks the necessary courage to take her life.

Krogstad assumes that *his* failure of nerve is a mirror of *hers*, that they are cowards as well as criminals beneath the skin. With the comfortable knowledge that his pressure on the Helmers can do no real harm to his secondary victim and that Torvald lacks the necessary moral fiber to resist, he escalates his demands on Nora. He has already rejected cash payment in favor of retaining his position in the bank. Now he wants more: he wants Nora to compel Torvald to promote him instantly, to create a new vacancy and install him as the second-in-command who actually *runs* the bank. His demand pushes Nora over the edge of reticence and indecision. This is the final challenge to Nora's courage, the goad that impels her flagging and uncertain will to accept responsibility for the consequences of her actions:

> NORA: Now I have the courage.
>
> KROGSTAD: You can't frighten mé! A precious pampered little thing like you . . .
>
> NORA: I'll show you! I'll show you!
>
> KROGSTAD: Under the ice, maybe? Down in the cold, black water? Then being washed up in the spring, bloated, hairless, unrecognizable . . .
>
> NORA: You can't frighten me.
>
> KROGSTAD: You can't frighten me, either. People don't do that sort of thing, Mrs. Helmer. (254)

Nora's leap of moral determination anticipates, once again, the defiant courage of Hedda Gabler in the face of incredulous male denials of her capacity for extraordinary action. The contemptuous sneer and the patronizing dismissal of the spoiled bourgeois doll are all subsumed in the phrase, reechoed in *Hedda Gabler* in Judge Brack's habitual taunt, "People don't do that sort of thing," that is, people do not rise above the norm of craven middle-class accommodation, do not behave heroically in an unheroic age. What Ibsen's women indicate, however, is a determination to do "that sort of thing" even in the face of a fearful reality. Dying, as Krogstad tells Nora, is not a romantic, sacrificial fantasy. Death is putrefaction and decay, ugliness and degradation. Nora may commit herself to death for bad and stupid reasons, but her motive does not detract from the courage it takes to contemplate a horrible death by drowning.

One by one Krogstad subverts the romantic ideals for which Nora will die until only Torvald remains. And until *he* demolishes himself in her estimation, she is willing to give her life for him. "*Gør så ingen dumhelder,*" Krogstad warns her (59); "Don't do anything stupid." His skeptical, contemptuous view of Torvald provides the vital dramatic counterpoint to Nora's blind trust in the "miraculous."

It is a mistake to think of Krogstad as a melodramatic image of unregenerate human nature, the sum total of villainous psychological deficiencies. He exists in a very clearly defined social and economic context: he is the creature formed by pietistic self-righteousness as a moral warning against offending its proprieties. Treat a man like a cur and, like Shylock, he will sooner or later bare his fangs. The Torvalds of the world have given Krogstad no quarter, shown no compassion for his children, and his bitterness derives from an intimate knowledge of the frail foundation upon which such social pillars rest—"There, but for the grace of God . . ." Ironically, ever since their school days, Krogstad has observed the hidden side of Torvald's personality, and he knows that behind the mask of the inflexible bank manager there lurks a spineless, morally accommodating pragmatist who will act in his own best interest when push comes to shove.

Krogstad is as narrowly confined in the commercial dolls' house as Nora is in the domestic dolls' house, is subject to the same petty exercise of authority, and is shaped by the same pressures to conform to type. Krogstad's parting salvo identifies Torvald as their common enemy and clarifies his motive in striking out against this incarnation of social injustice and indifference: "And don't forget: it's him who is forcing me off the straight and narrow again, your own husband!

That's something I'll never forgive him for" (254). What is remarkable about Krogstad is that in the last act of the play he abandons the tactics of retaliation and displays the greater power of "*hjertelag*" in his response to the individuals who make up the social world. In this play about transformations, Krogstad's capacity for change and moral recovery is perhaps the most significant mirror image of Nora's metamorphosis of spirit.

KROGSTAD'S METAMORPHOSIS

The details of Krogstad's wretched private life come sharply into focus in his scene with Mrs. Linde, which is a mirror for the dolls' house marriage and a gloss on Nora's sacrificial fantasies. "Let's talk," says Mrs. Linde, anticipating the Helmers' great reckoning at the end of the evening: both couples come to terms with each other, understand the dynamics of their relationship, and seek out alternatives to dollydom and the death of spirit in the middle-class commercial world.

Krogstad begins their interview by accusing Mrs. Linde of heartlessness and subordinating human feeling to economic consideration, love to money. Her response reveals the predicament of the dependent woman. The poor, she argues, burdened with responsibility, cannot afford to marry for love and must choose against the inclination of the heart no matter if it violates humanity. But even as she acknowledges necessity she questions her own justification. Life has now taught her the vanity of self-sacrifice and the need for caution and consideration. She will never sacrifice herself again, never humiliate herself to benefit another—not even Krogstad. He coolly assumes she will withdraw from the position at the bank, but she refuses to secure a questionable advantage for him by jeopardizing her own security.

Mrs. Linde offers Krogstad not sacrifice, but alliance: a life of mutual support, a joining of forces in which individual need is not subordinated to social or sexual expectations, and where strength derives from channeling energy and work into a common enterprise. In a startling reversal of traditional roles, *she* proposes to *him*, not marriage in a dolls' house state of dependency, but a form of "*sam-livet*": a "living together" in a reciprocity of equally balanced interests. She wants "*glæde*" (67) of life, the "joy" that has been precluded by narrow self-interest and the emptiness of her lonely existence, and she locates life's joy in human connections, in children who need a mother and a man who needs her. Krogstad momentarily mistakes her motives: "It's only a woman's hysteria," he suggests, "wanting to be all magnanimous and self-sacrificing" (264). But Mrs. Linde is not the hysterical type, and, as she points out, "When you've sold yourself *once* for other people's sake, you don't do it again" (265). She is no Nora for whom magnanimous self-sacrifice is still gloriously romantic, and the insubstantial fantasy of Nora's grand redemptive gesture, reflected in the cynical mirror of bitter experience, begins to look remarkably hysterical.

The capacity for terrible destruction inherent in sexual relationships is matched, in Ibsen's mirrored pair, by an equal capacity for creative change. Human connections are a matter of elective affinities. Who knows what sort of man Krogstad may have become were he married to Kristine Linde? Both seem to regard marriage as a form of chemical compound in which the constitutive ingredients lose their negative charge and recombine into entirely different substances. Krogstad could still become a different person through his alliance to a woman with courage enough to accept his tarnished reputation and faith enough in his essential goodness, however much it has been obscured beneath the grind of economic survival. The very basis of the play's existential optimism is "*at blevet en anden*" (67)—"to become another sort of human being"—a belief in humankind's ability to change, and a trust in the deep structure of man's moral nature. This is the concept implicit in Mrs. Linde's untranslatable phrase "*grundlaget i Dem*" (68), as she acknowledges strata of buried decency within Krogstad's definitive self; "I have faith," she says, "in what, deep down, you are" (265). It is a faith that spreads throughout the text and touches every human life in Ibsen's play.

Men driven by despair define themselves in vicious actions. We come to realize this about Krogstad in the early sections of the play:

the blackmailer has inconsistent flashes of heartfelt feeling. With a context in Mrs. Linde's trust and love, his "better self" (in Archer's phrase) begins to surface, he acknowledges his vindictive blow against the Helmers, and he agrees to retract his letter.

But, Mrs. Linde reneges on her promise to get the letter back for Nora, because circumstances have changed her mind. She has seen the joylessness of the dolls' house world, mired in fantasy and subterfuge and filled with pain and lies and self-delusion. If she can precipitate the sort of honest, open confrontation of husband and wife that has transformed *her* life, perhaps the Helmers too could understand each other more fully and change *theirs*. "*Hvilken vending! Ja, hvilken vending!*" (69) she cries as Krogstad hurries off to return the incriminating documents; "What a change of fortune! Yes, what a change of fortune." Yet in the mirror of the Krogstad/Linde peripeteia, the stuff of all comic resolutions, we see reflected the vastly different change of fortune that galvanizes the Helmers into life even as it wreaks tragic havoc in the dolls' house.

DR. RANK

In the tight symbolic structure of *A Doll's House* Krogstad is himself reflected off the other characters in the play—rather ponderously, as it turns out, in the affinity forced upon us by Dr. Rank's diagnosis of Krogstad's moral invalidism in terms of his own physical condition: "*bedærvet i karakter-rødderne*" (25); "rotten to the very core of his nature." The physician, dying of a pathological condition of the spine, reads his own corruption with sardonic bitterness into the state of the social world and anatomizes its structures as relentlessly as he probes his own terminal affliction. Bitter at the injustice of life, Dr. Rank's judgment becomes a self-reflexive comment on his own morbidity, and the correlation he implies between ethical and physical degeneration takes no account of the crucial difference between a remediable and a chronic affliction. His morally indignant response to Krogstad's very existence is based on the assumption that he knows, better than Nora, how society functions. There is nothing of the well-made play's *raisonneur* in this physician, none of the steadiness and wholeness of vision traditionally associated with the chorus of reliable doctors in the Dumas tradition. Dr. Rank's view of society is as unbalanced in its puritanism as Nora's view is in her insouciance: "What do I care about your silly old society?" she retorts (219), popping a macaroon into his mouth to sweeten the cynicism that she cannot bear to contemplate. If, indeed, she is Krogstad's counterpart in the hospital ward of society, she must stand accused of the same moral disease and suffer the same sort of enforced quarantine, and this sort of generalized thinking is more infectiously dangerous than the social typhus that Dr. Rank would like to extirpate.

Doctor Rank is the presiding spirit of this death-infected play, the incarnation of what it means to die in the midst of life's enchanting pleasures and Ibsen's most eloquent spokesman of the horror of the disintegrative process. In her scene of love and death with Dr. Rank, Nora stands in the presence of her own mortality, and in his despair at the nothingness and emptiness that assails existence, she confronts the meaningless oblivion of death in a world stripped of the tradition of Christian consolation. Death is not merely an event, immersion beneath the ice; it is a process of *"opløsning"* (51); of "disintegration and decomposition." As Dr. Rank lives through the horror of the physical stages he must endure, Nora's psychic *"opløsning"* comes slowly into focus. Her doll-self compounded of the false assumptions and delusive values of the doll's house world is dying. But, for all its superficiality, the doll's house is a very real world, and for Nora to deprive herself of its comforting certainties is to commit herself to a process as harrowing as Dr. Rank's. The central, dynamic movement of this scene, as I have already suggested, is Nora's illuminating flash of moral consciousness when, casting aside the perverse sexual maneuvers of the doll, she gives up all hope of extricating herself from death by exploiting Dr. Rank's affections, and her fate becomes as ineluctable as his.

Rank faces death with a grim sardonic humor, with a romantic and self-dramatizing bravado that strikes Nora as *"urimelig"* (51);

"absurd." But beneath Rank's joking is a deep vein of despair, a sense of the injustice of inherited disease and the cruel retribution in the gene: "Why should I suffer for another man's sins? What justice is there in that? Somewhere, somehow, every single family must be suffering some such cruel retribution" (245). The deterministic vision expands from the particular to the general until no family is exempt from its operation. The idea that rottenness is passed, like a kind of moral syphilis, from father to daughter and so on to the children, transforming dolls' houses into houses of contagion, is forced on Nora both by her friend and her husband, and she too readily accepts the notion. Her immediate response is to make light of the horror and so deny it. But even in trivializing the source of Rank's spinal syphilis by referring to his father's menu of sinful delicacies, Nora calls to mind the sadness of forfeiting life's pleasures before repletion and, for a brief moment, they share the pity of their common fate. It may be that, for a split second, each sees the other as a desire forever relinquished, a love abandoned before enjoyed. Dr. Rank is the man she would rather be with, as she later admits. Being with Torvald is rather like being with her father. There is a fleeting recognition here of real sexual attraction, which leads, with disastrous effect, to Nora's near seduction of Rank and his embarrassing declaration of a great romantic love.

Nora sees in Rank the mirror of her own inevitable death—not merely its sacrificial and romantic side, but the possibility of finality and forgetfulness, the empty place soon ignored or filled by the first person who comes along. All the sadness of dying fills their last scene together in act 3, with Dr. Rank's elegiac farewell to a world worth the leave-taking, and Nora's long goodbye after dancing the tarantella. Both have arrived at the moment of *"visshed"* (74); complete and confident "certainty." Nora learns from Dr. Rank's stoical acceptance of necessity how to face death without hysteria. Her last gesture of sympathetic affinity with her companion in life and death is to light his last cigar, a moment that rekindles the poignant memory of what each has lost in the other: *"ild"* (75); the sustaining "fire," the light, the ardor of a joyful life. The echoing pattern of their last lines of dialogue establishes the final mirror image in which each reflects the other:

NORA: Sleep well, Dr. Rank.

RANK: Thank you for that wish.

NORA: Wish me the same.

RANK: You? All right, if you want me to. . . . Sleep well. And thanks
        for the light. (272–73)

The rest of the play makes clear that this mirror in which Nora
is reflected, like all the others, ultimately emphasizes the *obverse* image—Ibsen's habitual *tvertimod,* his "contradictory" point of view.
Against Dr. Rank's spirit of diagnostic certainty, Nora commits herself
to possibility, to the transformative power of change even in a state of
terrible uncertainty. For Rank, change leads only to degeneration and
death, whereas for Nora, change offers a metamorphosis of intellect
and spirit. Rank looks at society with the inflexible gaze of absolute
certainty and finds it as hopelessly determined as his own physical
condition, but Nora is not delimited by his vision of unavoidable
necessity.

Even though her departure may be a form of death, Rank's vision
of disintegration and the slow process of decay is countermanded in
Nora's experience by the emergence of the woman from the socially
constructed doll. At every disintegrative stage of the wooden plaything, there is a reintegration of the autonomous woman, and the pain
of the doll's death is held in a delicate balance with the new and difficult life of Nora's self-sufficiency. Creating another identity simultaneously requires a relinquishment of the old and comfortable
certainties, the protective mask one wears to face the world. The emergent self, unshaped and vulnerable, must find its consolation in the
possibility of *becoming* its own essential creation by vigilant warfare
against the Trolls that lurk in the valves of the heart and the folds of
the brain—Dr. Rank's demons of despairing certainty, of hope eternally deferred, of unalterable circumstance, of death in life determined
by inflexible social codes. "Making life means making trouble," writes
Shaw in *Pygmalion,* his version of this myth of spiritual metamorphosis, and for Nora this is the antidote for death.

8

"The Problem of Women": *Nora and Mrs. Linde*

On the occasion of his seventieth birthday in May 1898, Ibsen demonstrated his reputation for contradiction and contrariness. To an enthusiastic attempt by the Norwegian Society for Women's Rights to claim his active partisanship, he uttered this crusty response: "I thank you for your toast, but must disclaim the honour of having consciously worked for women's rights. I am not even quite sure what women's rights really are. To me it has been a question of human rights. And if you have read my books carefully you will realize that. Of course it is incidentally desirable to solve the problem of women; but that has not been my whole object."[1] This is Ibsen at his most disingenuous. "The problem of women" is clearly a central, not merely a peripheral issue in *A Doll's House,* and I imagine in his rejoinder he was overreacting to the tendency among his champions to reduce the complex analysis of freedom in his plays about women to the politics of women's liberation.

If one understands "the problem of women" in strictly political terms, Norwegian working-class women had already broken the stony ground of equal rights for their middle-class sisters and the women's movement was well under way long before the advent of *A Doll's*

House. The grinding poverty of the early 1800s had forced women into the labor force, and the Storting, the Norwegian parliament, had made it possible for women to find both employment and protection within their work. It may be of small consolation to feminists to discover that, by 1845, Norwegian women had acquired the legal status of minor males, but however slowly the struggle proceeded, it achieved its gradual victories with little of the trauma that characterized the Women's Suffrage movement in England. Inheritance rights for women were secured in 1854, the right to university education in 1882, and a major victory for legal equality was won in 1888—10 years too late for Nora—when married women finally gained control over their own funds. *A Doll's House* may not be a "votes for women" sort of play (and Ibsen's crusty speech in 1898 clearly disclaims any tendentious issues in his writing), but *ufrihet*—the "unfree" condition of middle-class women—is of major concern in all his drama and encompasses the most crucial moral, psychological, and existential ideas in the plays from *A Doll's House* to *When We Dead Awaken*.

It would be misleading, however, to regard *A Doll's House* as a militant blow against the institution of marriage. Read my play carefully, Ibsen might say to his modern feminist celebrants, and you will find a dialectical contradiction at its center, for Nora's slamming the door on the dolls' house must be seen in the dramatic context of Mrs. Linde's motives for reentering that secure domestic world, and to see the play as recommending domestic revolution is to miss its surprising *tvertimod*.

With the resurgence of the women's liberation movement in the late 1960s, there has been a tendency to read *A Doll's House* as propaganda once more, and Kate Millett's influential and persuasive *Sexual Politics* (1970) has claimed Ibsen for the militant sisterhood even more enthusiastically than did the Norwegian Society for Women's Rights some 80 years earlier. *A Doll's House*, Millett writes, is a blow against the patriarchy, and Nora is "the true insurrectionary of the sexual revolution ... battling the sexual politic openly and rationally ... [with her] band of revolutionaries."[2]

The sentiments are perfectly sincere, but Kate Millett's banners-

and-trumpets rhetoric seems inappropriate to Ibsen's play. The play's point is that there is *no* band of revolutionaries, *no* sisterhood to support Nora in her decision, and her one potential ally—the friend who escapes from her burden of intolerable freedom into the domestic world—provides the gloss, the *tvertimod,* on Nora's tragic impulse towards a lonely liberation. In the 1880s, Nora's door-slamming exit demanded explanation and defense. In the 1990s, however, it is Mrs. Linde's surprisingly accommodating choice to embrace marriage and the dolls' house that challenges the liberated feminists and that they tend to ignore as an aspect of the play's governing idea. For the meaning of *A Doll's House,* its definition of the "problem of women," is inseparable from Ibsen's dramatic vision of liberation in the life choices of *both* of his female protagonists.

In a sense, of course, Millett and the modern feminist critics are quite right about the political Ibsen. The idea of "liberty" in his drama is inseparable from the liberal ideology that inspired the revolutions that reshaped the social structure of Europe and America at the end of the eighteenth century, or from the liberal impulse in Norway that set the country free from Danish and Swedish control in 1814. "Liberation" is, undeniably, a key concept in nineteenth-century political thought, which modulates, with historical inevitability, from pure abstract theory to specific implication, from philosophic speculation to practical concerns. In 1859 John Stuart Mill wrote the essay "Liberty," and in 1869 he wrote the essay "Subjection of Women," one of the great formative influences on the women's movement in Norway. Similarly, Ibsen, in his first play, *Catiline,* an impassioned response to the European revolution of 1848, begins with politics, but his notes for *A Doll's House* and *Ghosts,* written some 30 years later, echo Mill's historical shift to the specific.

The issue of liberation no longer merely centered on politics, but on what Kate Millett would call "sexual politics": the spiritual disenfranchisement of women in a world dominated by an alien moral law, an alien conscience, and the structures of a system untempered by the woman's vision of experience: "A woman cannot be herself in contemporary society, it is an exclusively male society with laws drafted by men, and with counsel and judges who judge feminine conduct from the male point of view" ("Commentary," 436). Ibsen's sympathies with the women's movement are manifest, especially with the writing and ideas of Magdalene Thoresen (his wife's stepmother) and the novelist Camilla Collett. But the polemical tone of his sexual politics is confined mainly to the notes for his plays. In his plays, as he told the Norwegian Society for Women's Rights, he is not a social philosopher but a poet for whom the politics of liberation have become the inspiration for his vision of the human predicament. He sees humankind as trapped, like Nora, between the seductive and soul-destroying security of her dolls' house and the frightening emptiness of the freedom that awaits her beyond the door. Political circumstance in *A Doll's House* is inseparable from the tragic implications of this particular woman's liberation, and the measure of her loss, as a free and emancipated spirit, is carefully gauged by the career of her mirror image, Kristine Linde, who enters the world of domestic security to seek a new definition of freedom within its confines.

DOLL MEETS NOT-DOLL

"Drama," writes H. D. F. Kitto, "is the art of significant juxtaposition,"[3] the balancing of images as if in a mirror, so that one image is both replication and obverse of the other, a simultaneous perspective and comment that shapes the form and meaning of the drama. Ibsen's pairing of his women in variously juxtaposed situations is a distinctive feature of his dramatic craft. Hedda and Thea Elvsted in *Hedda Gabler*, Rebekka and Beata in *Rosmersholm*, Maja and Irene in *When We Dead Awaken*, the list of pairings finally incorporates all those images in which one woman becomes the missing complement of the other—the demonic coupled with the domestic, the tempestuous woman with the ascetic, the dark with the fair. Nora and Mrs. Linde may be less adversarial in their coupling, less extreme in the aspects of femininity they embody, but together they constitute the *tvertimod* at the heart of the "problem of women," the eternally unreconciled needs and impulses that cry out for accommodation but that ultimately resist synthesis.

From the moment Mrs. Linde enters the play, the significant juxtapositions are clearly established: a displaced, prematurely aged traveller steps into the world of the comfortably well-established young wife, the subdued diffidence of the intruder nicely balancing the effervescent garrulity of the other. Nora chatters on about her snug and happy life, clearly enjoys playing "house" with this wintertime traveller, and assumes that Kristine has come to the city for a little Christmas merrymaking. But the presence of this pale, thin, and miserable woman contradicts Nora's erroneous assumptions, and Nora blunders into her next miscalculation, mistaking Mrs. Linde's dejection for a type of grieving widowhood:

NORA: (*gently.*) Poor Kristine, of course you're a widow now.

MRS. LINDE: Yes, my husband died three years ago.

NORA: . . . Oh, you poor thing, what you must have gone through. And didn't he leave you anything?

MRS. LINDE: No.

NORA: And no children?

MRS. LINDE: No.

NORA: Absolutely nothing?

MRS. LINDE: Nothing at all . . . not even a broken heart to grieve over.

NORA: (*looks at her incredulously.*) But, Kristine, is that possible?

MRS. LINDE: (*smiles sadly and strokes* NORA'S *hair.*) Oh, it sometimes happens, Nora.

NORA: So utterly alone. How terribly sad that must be for you. I have three lovely children. (208)

What had begun as a physical juxtaposition of contrasting appearances now modulates into a pattern of contrasting images of womanhood. One by one, Mrs. Linde had shed the ties (and the roles that they imply) that confine the woman to the dolls' house and define the angel in the late Victorian home: the unloved and unloving husband is dead, which frees Kristine from Nora's role as wife; there are no children, which frees her from Nora's happily purposeful maternity; there is no house, no property, which frees Kristine from dollydom itself, from Nora's happy housekeeping in her bourgeois paradise.

"Doll" confronts "not-doll" in one of those momentous oppositions of binary types: Nora is aghast to discover Mrs. Linde's bitterness and indifference to her husband's death, and Mrs. Linde is gently compassionate in the face of Nora's apparent innocence about marital distress. This is one of Ibsen's superbly understated moments, one in which the actress has to find the precise subtextual nuance to register Nora's leap of consciousness, the revelation of *her* predicament in the mirror life of Mrs. Linde. Some women, indeed, do not love their husbands, and when this is consciously realized, as I think it is in this scene, the truth needs cushioning from the awful implications—the instability of domestic values, the shattering of life's secure foundations, and the utter aloneness of the woman stripped of the roles that have given her status, purpose, and function in the great dolls' house of the social world. It is not entirely clear when subconscious fear emerges as appalling knowledge for Nora, but in the first scene with Mrs. Linde Ibsen edges the contours of Nora's destiny with the clarity of a consummate mapmaker.

What is at issue, for actress and director and reader, is the balance between Nora's superficial cheeriness and the extent of her genuine misery, the precise measure of consciousness that she permits to seep through her defensive dolliness. How much truth is she willing to acknowledge? How aware is she of playing happy families? How desperate is she to suppress the "*død og pine*" (death and pain) beneath the pretense of domestic bliss? Her gasp of incredulity and her vision of the utter loneliness of the displaced woman is instantly countermanded by a packetful of verbal macaroons: what lovely children we have, how lucky we are to be moving up in the world, how happy we are to have masses of disposable income! "*Å, Kristine, hvor jeg føler mig let og lykkelig! Ja, for det er dog dejligt at have dygtig mange penge og ikke behøve at gøre sig bekymringer. Ikke sandt?*" (16); "Oh,

Kristine, I'm so happy and relieved. I must say its lovely to have plenty of money and not have to worry. Isn't it?" (209). At the end of the play Nora will *know* that this is a trite and cliché-ridden definition of what it means to be happy—*lykkelig*. But, during this scene, she is merely *relieved* to have the security of a good income and not to scrutinize her equation of plenty of money equals peace of mind.

Nora has invested too much in her marriage, and she has too much to lose. Proudly she recounts their rise from genteel civil service poverty to the middle-class security of bank management, her financial contribution to Torvald's resplendent career, and so on and so forth. What she recounts is a tissue of half-truths, suppressed information, and sentimentally remembered facts, the sort of fiction on which readers of Harlequin Romances thrive, and (we come to realize) the sort of self-deceiving illusion that sustains the rather tenuous stability of Nora's dolls' house. That dolls' house stands (we come to realize) on a foundation of small white lies and necessary self-delusions. "Dying father leaves money"; "pregnant mother sacrifices inheritance"; "selfless wife saves husband's life." Nora will return to her narrative later in the scene and substantially revise it. But the actress must find a slight touch of the fantastic, a deliberate effort at cover-up, even at this stage of Nora's conjured image of marvellous bliss in the dolls' house. Nora is responding, it seems to me, to the awful alternative that confronts her in the other woman.

"Tell me," she asks Mrs. Linde, "is it really true that you didn't love your husband? What made you marry him, then?" (211). The focus suddenly shifts to the reality of a woman trapped in a loveless marriage who has had, in a totally unsentimental way, to sacrifice *her* happiness to provide for a desperately sick mother and two younger brothers. Mrs. Linde is totally matter-of-fact in her account. All her choices were determined by need. But the drudgery of her life is over: the husband and the ailing mother are dead, and there is no need to play the wife, the servant, or the nurse; the brothers can fend for themselves, and there is no need to play the nanny, housekeeper, or surrogate mother.

Mrs. Linde is completely free from every one of the delimiting roles of nineteenth-century womanhood, whereas Nora, so ambiguously comfortable in an Edenic world sustained by deceit, half-conscious self-deception, and a willing collaboration in her own suppression, is momentarily envious of this free, unshackled state: "*Hvor du ma føle dig let*" (18); "What a relief you must find it" (211). But it is not relief or freedom from these roles that Mrs. Linde experiences at all. The opposite of dollydom is not woman's liberation, she indicates, but woman's unspeakable alienation from a world of necessary connections and relationships: "*Nej, du; bare så usigelig tom. Ingen at leve for mere*" (18); "No, Nora! Just unutterably empty. Nobody to live for any more" (211).

Life outside the dolls' house leaves a woman destitute, bitter, and frighteningly self-reliant in a way that makes all activity reductively egocentric and all motives merely forms of self-interest. "That's the worst thing about people in my position," Kristine tells Nora, "they become so bitter. One has nobody to work for, yet one has to be on the look-out all the time. Life has to go on, and one starts thinking only of oneself" (211). "*Egenkærlighed*"—that sense of selfish isolation from the well-being of others—is as appalling to Mrs. Linde as the psychic emptiness she feels, the social displacement, the existential redundancy—the sum total of Ibsen's dramatic image of alienation. Her despair surfaces again and again, particularly in her act 3 discussion with Krogstad, in phrases that typify the converse of Nora's dolls' house condition: "*Men nu står jeg ganske alene i verden, så forfærdelig tom og forladt*"; "But now I'm completely alone in the world, and feeling horribly empty and forlorn." "*At arbejde for sig selv, er jo ingen glæde i*"; "There's no pleasure in working only for yourself." "*Ingen at sørge over, og ingen at sørge for*"; "[I have] nobody to care about, and nobody to care for." Her isolation and loneliness are summed up, finally, in a harrowing metaphor of flotsam, an image taken over from Krogstad: "*Jeg sidder også som en skibbruden kvinde på et vrag*" (67); "And I am like a broken woman clinging to the wreck of her life" (264). Her need, clearly, is *to be needed,* to rediscover significance in the reciprocal impulses that inform relationships and bind families into creative and sustaining entities.

"The Problem of Women": Nora and Mrs. Linde

Even a dolls' house may be better than the nothingness of the world beyond it.

When, at the end of the play, Nora goes through an equally harrowing experience of self-dispossession and redefinition—in "full freedom" (285) as she insists—it becomes impossible to dissociate her liberated life from the context of shipwreck and alienation, the frustration of human needs, and the deprivation of psychological security that Mrs. Linde has so poignantly articulated. The free spirit who leaves the dolls' house of shattered values does so, just as Mrs. Linde had once entered Nora's cozy world, *"ganske alene"* (83); "utterly alone"—without vocation, without orientation or support, a black-garbed emblem of the devastation to which she has heroically committed herself. One leaves the dolls' house, not with trumpets and banners but with fear and trembling, because choosing liberation of this nature means looking into the face of death.

Mrs. Linde's superobjective in entering the Helmers' world of limited influence and small power is to find a niche for herself within it, to gain security through connection, to come in (as it were) from the cold. She admits this freely, and Nora undertakes to pull the necessary strings, and in the usual manner of exercising influence in the dolls' house—"oh-so-subtly," *"sa fint, sa fint"* (19)—she lulls Torvald into a good mood with her *"elskværdigthed"*; her special and "seductive charm." Sex rules where all else fails in the domestic realm, and Nora knows well how to gain her little advantages with the calculated maneuvering of a Victorian Cleopatra. Power must be exercised indirectly, cunningly, even if it entails demeaning herself in the process by doing her doll's performance.

Nora senses Mrs. Linde's condescending view of the doll-wife insulated against life's hardships and troubled by nothing more wearisome than her small domestic chores, and she hotly contradicts this appearance of uselessness and triviality by going over the ground, once more, of her great undertaking. She will match Kristine, point for point, in significant self-sacrifice. This is the moment, as in the *pièce bien fait*, of the momentous disclosure when the buried secret is finally revealed and time past floods time present. But two factors diminish the weight of the disclosure: Nora's motive for whispering the information so that Torvald remains in the dark, and her deliberate suppression (yet again) of vital information.

The "selfless wife saves husband" narrative gains immeasurably in dramatic impact as Nora fills in the details and embellishes them. Torvald would *never* have recovered from his debilitating illness but for her intervention. She raised a vast sum of money (she provides the precise sum in both forms of Norwegian currency, dollars and kroner), quite independently, in this revised version, of any help from her father. She refuses to disclose the source of her financing, except to dismiss with contempt the notion of a sweepstake—which would clearly detract from the glory of her achievement and compromise the extraordinary cleverness of her "business-mind"; her "*forretningsdygtighed*" (21). (The birdbrain/scatterbrain epithets that Torvald habitually uses to describe her are thrown into startling perspective by her disclosures, no matter how coy or exaggerated her account). Despite the fact that wives may not borrow without their husbands' knowledge and consent, she has managed to outmaneuver the legal restrictions on her contractual rights and belie the helplessness of the angel in the house. Clearly, there are only two ways for a woman to raise 4,800 kroner—sexually or illegally—and Nora teases Kristine with the dual possibilities—the power of the doll or the rashness of the petty criminal.

What becomes patently clear is that Nora's sexual power trips in the dolls' house are conscious ploys, manipulating roles she plays in full knowledge of alternative courses of action. We need to know why she continues, even after she has acquired business acumen and tough "masculine" dealing, to perpetuate the dolly game and suffer the humiliation of Torvald's patronizing sexual compliments. After all, as she tells Kristine later in the scene, one of her greatest satisfactions has had little to do with noble self-sacrifice or husband-saving: "But it was tremendous fun all the same, sitting there working and making money like that. It was almost like being a man" (216).

The "doll" and the "not-doll" seem strangely to vie for significance in Nora's self-evaluation. She prides herself on breaking out of the mold and the social-sexual stereotype while at the same time she thoroughly depends on her status as the doll in the dolls' house. In her resourcefulness and management of affairs she is *almost* like a man, but, as Ibsen indicates in his notes, an aspect of Nora's "problem" is that her ethical vision and her sense of natural law are not easily accommodated by the authoritarian structures of the male-dominated world. When Mrs. Linde fears the possibility of illegal rashness in Nora's raising of so much money, Nora replies with blithe indifference to the dictates of the law, "Is it rash to save your husband's life?" (214), the same tone of apparent naïveté with which, earlier on, she speaks of the widow's obligations to discharge her husband's debts: "If anything as awful as that did happen, I wouldn't care if I owed anybody anything or not," to which Torvald retorts, "Just like a woman!" (202–3). "She has committed a crime," says Ibsen, "and she is proud of it; because she did it for love of her husband and to save his life. But the husband, with his conventional views of honour, stands on the side of the law and looks at the affair with male eyes" ("Commentary," 437). Here, surely, is one reason for Nora's deliberate withholding of information from Torvald: she has an acute sense of how her motives, *as a woman*—at best scatterbrained, at worst criminally delinquent—would be evaluated by the conventional attitudes of male authority.

But this is only one among many possible reasons why the "doll" in Nora conceals so resolutely the almost manlike acumen of the "not-doll." Nora, indeed, provides reason after reason, peeling away the layers of the dolls' house even as she details its structure until her relationship with Torvald is fully revealed in all its devastating emptiness, although it is still papered over with the decorative veneer of "*vort skønne lykkelige hjem*" (22); "our pretty and happy home." Masculine prerogative must be maintained at whatever cost to the wife's autonomy, and to ensure the stability of the dolls' house Nora will submit to the petty tyranny of her husband's whims and fancies and dutifully protect his image as a household god. Torvald, therefore, cannot be taken into her confidence because her subterfuge would be exposed, because he would be furious at her for disobeying him and borrowing money, because she fears his uncompromising economic house rules, because she would put him under an obligation to her and compromise his chauvinistic pride: "it would be terribly embarrassing and humiliating for him if he thought he owed anything to me" (215). In short, she says, his knowing the truth would ruin her marriage and spoil her home life, and nothing would ever be the same again. Her strategy, therefore, is to maintain appearances even if it means concealing facts, living a lie, and playing a succession of roles that guarantee her security as a wife even while belittling her as an independent and resourceful human being. But she will not go along with this subterfuge forever. Timing is all. Nora will indeed reveal her dark secret to Torvald, but not before it becomes imperative for her to do so. This much she makes clear to Mrs. Linde, and the revelation of her motive fully reveals, at last, the tenuous and insecure nature of existence in the dolls' house:

MRS. LINDE: Are you never going to tell him?

NORA: (*reflectively, half-smiling.*) Oh yes, some day perhaps ... in many years time, when I'm no longer pretty as I am now. You mustn't laugh! What I mean of course is when Torvald isn't quite so much in love with me as he is now, when he's lost interest in watching me dance, or get dressed up, or recite. Then it might be a good thing to have something in reserve.... (*Breaks off.*) What nonsense! That day will never come. (215)

If *sex* is power in the dolls' house, then it is power of the most unstable kind. This power depends, as Nora indicates, on physical beauty that must inevitably wane, on maintaining a level of sexual intensity that will diminish, on being able (like Scheherazade) to hold the husband's interest by fascinating him forever. But how long can one exercise control by dancing, dressing up, and reciting? For all her confidence in "*elskværdigthed*," her accommodating "charm," she knows that this power is an essentially temporary means of securing her position, her sporadic gifts of cash, and her domestic will. What really lies behind the "selfless wife saves husband" romance is the desperate need "*at have noget i baghånden*" (22); the gambler's trick of "having something up the sleeve." Her dark secret is a form of self-protection against the frightful insecurity of life in the dolls' house and the loss of status and control as Torvald's ardor cools, and although she denies this eventuality, it clearly preys on her mind as the sad destiny of every angel in the house.

If Nora must keep Torvald in the dark to gain some future psychological advantage over him, then her motive for the great heroic deed disintegrates into a form of emotional blackmail (should the occasion for revealing the deed ever arise). There is no such impulse as disinterested decency in the dolls' house, no domestic ideal untainted by necessary self-interest. Women, spiritually disenfranchised and driven into cunning subterfuge to secure their place in the kingdom of masculine prerogative, play the roles that give them power despite the cost to their self-respect and dignity. For Nora, playing the role is a matter of habit and accommodation. Her behavior reflects the image of the featherbrained pet in Torvald's mind because she has consciously repressed the threatening alternative. She responds to the nauseous cant of Torvald's uxorious affection because she has traded a dangerous autonomy for the comfortable security of a life that reduces her to the status of a caged skylark. There is a willing suspension of her own human significance in the roles she plays, in the illusion she sustains of a domestic paradise, in the deceit and the half-truths that constitute the myth of the lovely and happy home. Every now and then, in her reflective and half-smiling moments, her fear and anxiety surface, only to be countermanded by denial or a rapid reversion to the picture-book visions of ideal marriage in cheap romantic fiction: "Oh God, what a glorious thought, Kristine! . . . being able to romp with the children, and making the house nice and attractive, and having things just as Torvald likes to have them! And then spring will soon be here, and blue skies. And maybe we can go away somewhere. I might even see something of the sea again. Oh yes! When you're happy, life is a wonderful thing!" (216). This systolic/diastolic rhythm is typical of Nora's consciousness. An overprotested determination to cling to the illusions she knows are delusory is punctuated with momentary shafts of barely conscious insight into her own discredited motivation.

LIBERATION AND ALIENATION

"The problem of women" in *A Doll's House*, then, centers on the significant juxtaposition of Nora and Mrs. Linde, "doll" and "not-doll" and the dialectics that make each a mirror image of the other. The play's structure finally reveals a vision of equally balanced deficiencies and desires, Ibsen's *tvertimod*, that dramatizes his highly ironic meditation on the theme of freedom. If life *outside* the dolls' house is seen as a hell of alienation and dispossession, then life *within* it is no more than an anti-Eden of lies and self-delusion. If the alienated woman craves the security of the dolls' house to fulfill an indispensable emotional need, then her domesticated sister yearns for liberation from its subjugation to fulfill an equally insistent existential necessity. Each looks to the other as the paradigm of the desired condition, and each sees in the mirror the dreadful consequences of desires satisfied. Security and liberation demand satisfaction in equal measure, but the two seem to remain eternally unreconcilable: security (in Nora's experience) means trading autonomy for a facile happiness, whereas liberation (in Mrs. Linde's experience) means trading human connection for a lonely freedom. The structure, as a whole, seems to cry out for a miracle, a synthesis of contraries that could reconcile the genuinely sustaining possibilities of the dolls' house with the emancipation of human spirit from the repressive implications of its operation. The play ends with an interchange of roles: the erstwhile "doll" steps into the world of the "not-doll," and the alienated woman steps into the dolls' house. But "the problem of women" seems to remain, somewhat equivocally, unresolved in Ibsen's later drama. The heroines of *Rosmersholm* and *Hedda Gabler* continue to share in Nora's strenuous quest for liberating values within the constraints of social life, and struggle against the limitations heaped on the aspiring spirit by the failures and insufficiencies of personal life.

"The Problem of Women": Nora and Mrs. Linde

Irony and equivocation are the distinctive qualities of Ibsen's dramatic *tvertimod* that leave the issues open even after the final curtain falls. Is Nora a "liberated woman" when she slams the door on the dolls' house? Does Mrs. Linde become a "doll" when she enters so unabashedly into Krogstad's family? The *tvertimod* says, simultaneously, "yes" and "no", and to understand the dénouement of *A Doll's House* is to understand something of the complexity of Ibsen's deliberation on the theme of freedom in his later plays and the tragic ambiguities that characterize his liberated heroines. If Kate Millett takes a decidedly optimistic "yes" view of Nora as the new woman, other critics of Ibsen's women are far more realistically somber in their evaluation of her career. "We might remind ourselves," writes Inga-Stina Ewbank (a strong voice from the "no" camp), "that [Ibsen's] plays resolve themselves either in the tragic impossibility of his women characters being liberated into anything other than death, or else in a liberation so tenuous and self-defeating that, as with Nora, it has been felt to be a fate worse than death."[4] Ibsen's dénouements are a curious conflation of exhilaration and catastrophe, and his inevitable linking of a breath-taking freedom with trembling and the fear of death points to a paradoxical definition of women's liberation that transcends all sexual politics.

One of the most illuminating glosses on this aspect of Ibsen's dramatic vision is Eric Fromm's *The Fear of Freedom*,[5] an enquiry, partly psychological and partly political, into the capitulation of free individuals to the rising tide of fascism and Nazism in Europe in the 1930s and 1940s. Why, he asks, do people surrender their souls so willingly for security? Why is freedom a condition so fearful to sustain that mankind is prepared to trade it for illusions of well-being? (Fromm, 15). Society, he argues, is (like the dolls' house) a paradisal haven where one surrenders a lonely autonomy to communal control and where the pain of isolated selfhood is assuaged by surrender to the values of the world. To dissent is to be cast out of paradise. And the fall from this Eden is experienced as a fall into freedom that asserts individuality at the cost of security, that simultaneously liberates and alienates, and that frees man from his determined state but leaves him anxious, uprooted, uncertain:

He is alone and free, yet powerless and afraid. The newly won freedom appears as a curse; he is free *from* the sweet bondage of paradise, but he is not free *to* govern himself, to realize his
individuality. "Freedom from" is not identical with positive freedom, with "freedom to." . . . This growing individuation means
growing isolation, insecurity, and thereby growing doubt concern-
ing one's role in the universe, the meaning of one's life, and with all
that a growing feeling of one's own powerlessness and insignifi-
cance as an individual. (Fromm, 28–29)

To understand the dolls' house as a place of "sweet bondage," as
a demiparadise, is to appreciate the pain of having to leave it. For to
be *free from* paradise is to be lost, not liberated, alienated, not reshaped as an autonomous being. Mrs. Linde, as I have suggested, ar-
ticulates the devastating "freedom from" condition that she would
willingly forfeit in favor of the bonds of belonging and the intolerable
burden of liberation that she would exchange to assuage her loneliness. To achieve this without submission to masculine prerogative,
without the abnegation of autonomy and self-respect, is one way of
liberating the doll even within the confines of the dolls' house, and,
perhaps in her relationship with Krogstad, Mrs. Linde will achieve a
minor miracle. There remains that one unexplored possibility in the
play: Mrs. Linde may, after the awful experience of her own and
Nora's failure, transform the dolls' house into a home. She may, in a
marriage based on trust and honesty and genuine human connection,
be more essentially free than Nora, who must step into the fallen
world as a tragically isolated and inexperienced being.

For Mrs. Linde is now *free to* reshape her life, redefine her relationships, and correlate her needs with the needs of a lover and a family. There is nothing heroic or tragic about her accommodation, for
her resolution (if one can endorse it as such) is the stuff of comedy, a
confirmation of family, society, and state as the source of well-being
and the good life. Hers is a vision of the very ordinary domestic freedom that Ibsen will validate in *The Lady from the Sea* and ask us to
accept as the "miracle" of a good marriage. But there is neither exhilaration nor catastrophe in the happy ending that I have just extrapo-

lated for Mrs. Linde. Nora, in significant juxtaposition, has won her *freedom from*, in all its perilous distress, freedom from all the negative factors in the dolls' house, but, ineluctably, a concomitant freedom from its deepest satisfactions: the love of husband, the sweetness of children, and the moments of genuine happiness. She is *free from* but not yet *free to.* Ibsen leaves her at that moment of tragic crisis when the exhilarating strength of intellectual clarification and positive decision is counterbalanced by the catastrophic insecurity of her hard-won liberation.

9

"Bird and Birdcatcher": Nora and Torvald

"*Er det lærkefuglen, som kvidrer derude?*" (9) is Torvald's first line in the play, simultaneously loving and demeaning, a mixture of genuine pleasure and irritating cuteness on hearing Nora return to their love nest: "Is that my little sky-lark chirruping out there?" (201). It is not the decor of the dolls' house that creates the claustrophobia in the play, but the rhetoric, the baby talk ("little sweet-tooth") that reinforces Nora's propensity to childishness, the nursery jargon ("my pretty little pet squirrel") that reduces her careful domestic budgeting to playful hoarding, and the dreadful neologisms that encage her in Torvald's lumbering attempts at playful moralizing: "*spillefuglen*" (10); the "wastrel-bird," the "spendswift," the songster who squanders cash. As the first scene unfolds, so her incarceration in his language becomes more and more oppressive.

Torvald treats his wife like a naughty child, playfully tweaking her ear and scolding her about the macaroons. He buys his pet out of the sulks by rewarding her with cash, and she twitters and squeals and plays the game, tells him childish lies about the macaroons, and plays the role of "*spillefuglen*" and "*lærkefulglen*" and "*sanglærken*" when, in Blake's indignant words, her situation "puts all Heaven in a rage."

"Bird and Birdcatcher": Nora and Torvald

Ironically of course, the *real* Nora, the self-reliant, levelheaded economist, is completely smothered beneath the patronizing domestic banter. What is equally ironic is that *she* traps him by her acquiescence in these featherbrained images as fatally as *he* traps her in his cant. Each is held prisoner in a deadly cycle of mutually reinforcing images. Ibsen pairs "Fugl og Fuglefænger" ("Bird and Birdcatcher"), which is the title of a poem that Ibsen wrote nearly 30 years before *A Doll's House*. Although the poem does not mesh detail for detail with Ibsen's play, its frightening allegory encompasses an important dimension of the Helmers' destructive relationship. In the first person narrative, the poem tells of a boy who builds a pretty pine twig birdcage and (unlike Torvald) maliciously torments his bird-victim until he grows bored with his own petty cruelty and decides to free his prisoner. But life and freedom are not easily repossessed. In its bid for the sunlight, the bird's wings fail and it whirls downwards and is crushed. At this point the boy-narrator's point of view is superceded by the omniscient gaze of one who sees *the boy* as a bird, constricted in his own narrow cage and as trapped and confused in his predicament as his victim has been:

> *Også ham et øje stirrer*
> *skræmsomt på igennem gitret.*
> *Dette blik hans sind forvirrer;*
> *rædsel har ham gennemsitret.*

> *Og når han på gab tror ane*
> *vinduet, som til frihed bringer,*
> *dratter han med brudte vinger,*
> *bums, ifra sin stængte bane.*

> At him too an eye is glaring
> terror through the bars about him
> He's confounded by this staring,
> feels the quake of fear throughout him.

> He too for a window dashes
> when he glimpses freedom's gateway;

but his wing is broken straightway;
down in checked mid-flight, he crashes.[1]

The act of imprisoning imprisons us. This idea, rather than one of retribution, shapes the vision of Ibsen's poem and its image of the social structure that encages us within the very systems we endorse. Torvald, trapping Nora in her role as *"spillefugl"* or wastrel-bird, is in turn defined by the culture that imprisons *him*. By obliging her to play the "bird," his role of "birdcatcher" becomes inevitable, just as the domestic construct of the sexually winsome and featherbrained wife presupposes the presence of its corollary in the manly protector whose wisdom and heroism ensure her safety. If Torvald insists on seeing Nora as "Barbie," she in turn comes to see him as "Ken," and each plays up to the other's social, domestic, and sexual expectations, maintaining a façade that gradually hardens into a kind of half-life.

DOLLYDOM

The nature of dollydom in the play involves role-playing that becomes so habitual it belies the reality beneath the fabricated structure, so wooden that insecure and suffering human beings disappear beneath the puppetplay in which they are trapped. Neither Nora nor Torvald helps the other to realize his or her humanity or ease his or her unhappiness. Nora is as much to blame as Torvald because she never questions his crass authority, never sees the pitiful insecurity that manifests itself in arrogance or the small-mindedness that masquerades as moral superiority. Torvald is certainly no brute, but his blinkered vision and parochial values ensure the perpetuation of every social prejudice, every ill-conceived opinion, every unquestioned cliché of late nineteenth-century society. The pity is that Nora thinks of him as God, honors his morality as Gospel, and obeys his whims and fancies as if they were the Decalogue.

"Hell," says one of Jean-Paul Sartre's characters, "is other people."[2] That is, we *become* the roles and identities that "other people" prescribe for us, and others have the power to delimit our infinite human capacities and reduce us to the raw material of their own needs. If we permit this to happen, we do so because we exist in a condition of mutual dependency, anxious to have our best conception of ourselves objectively endorsed by some external source. So we trade autonomy for approval and independent selfhood for social conditioning, and we make a hellish compromise with "other people" who have the power, by our acquiescence, to appropriate our selfhood and transform us into the sorts of creatures they choose to see.

But "hell is other people" only insofar as we conform to their reductive image and permit that image to substitute for the defining quality of our being. Hell is patently *not* other people as long as we are able to define the existential basis of our own personality and refuse to play the "bird" to the "birdcatchers" of the world. The problem for the doll is that her conditioning has been relentless. Nora, for the most part, sees "Nora" as other people see her—as a construct shaped by the nexus of family relationships and determined by the forces of heredity, environment, and the prejudices of cultural attitudes towards women that have been reinforced by the tenets of the church and the law. When, at the end of the play, Nora discovers that her primary duty is to her *self—"pligterne imod mig selv"* (84)—her revelation is an acknowledgment that such selfhood exists beyond the wife and mother images of *les autres*. She has discovered a sentiment of necessary self-regard, a difficult autonomy that must not be confused with the ruthless egotism of the "me" generation.

All relationships, Ibsen implies in another of his plays, are versions of a universal bird and birdcatcher game in which we willingly collaborate, alternating roles in controlled exchanges of power that trade in mutually supporting images. This sardonic view is dramatized in the meeting of old friends in *John Gabriel Borkman*, in which each character is the repository of the other's ideal image of himself, but "hellishly" unwilling, at this point in their relationship, to sustain the mutual delusion:

BORKMAN: Haven't you sat here feeding me with hope, and trust and confidence? Wasn't that all lies?

FOLDAL: It wasn't a lie while you believed in my vocation. As long as you believed in me, I believed in you.

BORKMAN: Then we've been deceiving each other. And perhaps deceiving ourselves too.

FOLDAL: Isn't that the basis of friendship, John Gabriel?

BORKMAN: (*smiles bitterly.*) Yes. To deceive . . . That's friendship. You're right. I've had the experience once before.
(*John Gabriel Borkman*, 8:191)

The Helmers' marriage is like this friendship but without the old friends' wry consciousness of the game. The Helmers' delusions are far more deeply entrenched, each believing so tenaciously in the doll identity of the other that the *idea* has replaced the living reality.

The little white lies about the macaroons are symptomatic of a much greater lie, the life lie of the "happy marriage" that, like all the life lies in Ibsen's plays, stands poised on the knife-edge of sustaining illusion and a neurotic withdrawal from reality. They have been deceiving each other for years and, in the process, deceiving themselves. But only Nora, in sporadic moments of painful introspection, comes to recognize the peculiar hellishness of their dolls' house paradise. The momentum of the play derives from a succession of epiphanies through which Nora recasts the contents of her mind, and from her final transformation from lifeless perfect doll-wife in her husband's imagination to her definition of authentic selfhood.

At the end of the play, Nora levels a bitter indictment against the world of male authority and the tenets of male dogma that, she argues, have conditioned her existence from childhood:

At home, Daddy used to tell me what he thought, then I thought the same. And if I thought differently, I kept quiet about it, because he wouldn't have liked it. He used to call me his baby doll, and he played with me as I used to play with my dolls. Then I came to live in your house. . . . What I mean is: I passed out of Daddy's hands into yours. You arranged everything to your tastes and I acquired the same tastes. Or I pretended to . . . I don't really know . . . I think it was a bit of both, sometimes one thing and sometimes the other. (280)

Consciously embodying the social/sexual stereotype (yet subconsciously rejecting it), Nora has retained only a tenuous understanding of herself and the world. All her views are Torvald's, as they had once been her father's, and she has accepted without question a whole range of moral and economic opinions, genetic theories, unsubstantiated statistical pronouncements, and the proprietorial sexual attitudes that bolster Torvald's chauvinistic self-image as her heroic birdcatcher.

MALE DOLLYDOM

Torvald's utterances are a Golden Treasury of platitude and superstition, a lexicon of ill-formed ideas expressed as punitive morality or congratulatory self-righteousness, and his stringent interpretation of the law is ultimately inseparable from his own moral fanatacism: "Many a man might be able to redeem himself, if he honestly confessed his guilt and took his punishment" (232); "Practically all juvenile delinquents come from homes where the mother is dishonest" (233); "My dear little Nora, there is a considerable difference between your father and me. Your father's professional conduct was not entirely above suspicion. Mine is. And I hope it's going to stay that way as long as I hold this position" (242). Torvald's high ethical tone is particularly in evidence when he discusses Nora's father (whose carelessness with money, Torvald proclaims, is genetically transferable) and the sad career of Krogstad (whose carelessness with grammar is morally untenable). And although, at moments of penetrating insight into her husband's character Nora is able to see the incredible pettiness masquerading as morality, she is easily persuaded to accept the posturing of the birdcatcher as the real thing: the heroic husband displacing the small-minded bully in the rhetoric of grand romantic fiction.

With Nora's second appeal to Torvald's mercy, the staunch moralist begins to crack a little, only to reveal the pusillanimity beneath his apparent tough mindedness. For Torvald would be a laughing stock at the bank if he allowed himself to be swayed by his wife. Pride, pomposity, and loss of face are what really matter to him. In a vengeful response to her charge that he has treated Krogstad with petty vindictiveness, Torvald dashes off a note of instant dismissal, and then he lapses into his other mode of being in the dolls' house and becomes the image of the ideal male that Nora is only too ready to endorse: "I forgive you all the same, because it is rather a sweet way of showing how much you love me. (*He takes her in his arms.*) This is how things must be, my own darling Nora. When it comes to the point, I've enough strength and enough courage, believe me, for whatever happens. You'll find I'm man enough to take everything on myself" (244).

To Torvald being "man enough" means conforming to every nineteenth-century stereotype of male authority and playing the social pillar and paterfamilias by the unwritten textbook of how "real" men should function in the world. "Like Nora," writes Evert Sprinchorn, "he has been formed or conditioned by social conventions and attitudes and made to play a part that by nature he is perhaps not well suited for. . . . Torvald turns out to have been the doll all along."[3]

Respectability and defensive face-saving are everything to Torvald, who has the temperament of the scrupulous businessman, the ministry's trusted financial investigator, and whose virtues are inseparable from his vices. His honesty is so excessive that it borders on moral persecution, and his diligence is so extreme that he turns his home into an extension of this office.

Krogstad, of course, is one of *les autres,* and he sees the other side of Torvald and recognizes him as the antithesis of the sacrificial hero. In Krogstad's vocabulary, Torvald is "*du*": known and familiar, a fellow student, short on courage, neither more respectable nor more competent than himself. Push Torvald to the wall, Krogstad intimates to Nora, and her husband will capitulate without a murmur.

If Krogstad has been victimized by Torvald's temperament, then so has Nora. Her "happy home" is as tyrannically controlled as the bank: governed by ground rules that forbid certain domestic activities (like mending) to be performed in his presence, dominated by his arbitrary tastes and preferences (embroidery is a more graceful activity for women than knitting), and reigned over in the smallest of everyday details (even the letter box is kept under constant surveillance).

He has also been formed and conditioned by Nora's *licensing* of his male-doll role. He is the birdcatcher caught in the cultural system and sustained in his illusions by the bird's deliberate suppression of her capacity for flight and her apparent acquiescence in his authoritarian control. Nora has in fact been "man enough" to take everything on herself in a crisis, and it is *she* who has been the support of the family and the unobtrusive stage manager behind the dolls' house set of the "happy home." The macho posturing, the imperious attitudes, and the condescending rhetoric are all preposterous. Nora could eclipse them with a wink, but she chooses not to. The stability of her marriage and the security of her home depend on the nurturing of the lie, and, like Foldal and Borkman, she accepts deception as the basis of her marriage. She believes in the romantic hero as a necessary defense against the terrible alternative, and suffering the petty tyrannies of the domestic bully becomes part of the psychopathology of her daily life.

Like *Othello's* Desdemona, Nora sees her husband's visage in her mind—sees him, in other words, *as he ideally sees himself,* as the essentially manly man whose love bears it out even to the edge of doom: "Oh, my darling wife, I can't hold you close enough. You know, Nora . . . many's the time I wish you were threatened by some terrible danger so I could risk everything, body and soul, for your sake" (274). "*Liv og blod og alt*" (76); he offers to spill his "life's blood" for her in a fantastic romantic "*libestod.*" This dream is as trite and conventional and unconvincing as Nora's "selfless wife saves husband" dream, but it affirms her vision of an ideal husband and displaces the constant reality she prefers to ignore. But Nora does *not* share with Desdemona the ability to see, with compassion and charity, the fallible man beneath the inflated rhetoric, the ordinary husband behind the exotic bridegroom: "Nay, we must think men are not gods, / Nor of them look for such observancy / As fits the bridal." (*Othello* 3.4.148–50).

Torvald's "observancy," as it turns out, consists of an equal measure of romantic sacrifice and romantic eroticism: the Savior and the sexual fantasist alternate in fairly rapid and ironic succession. When the tarantella arouses desire in him, he virtually drags Nora away from the party to take her to bed. This scene matches, in embarrassment and inappropriate sexual behavior, Nora's titillation of Rank with the silk stockings. While *she* is preparing for death *he* is preparing for sex, and the incongruity is heightened by his need to seduce her in a state of mild inebriation. There is nothing in his love talk, now, of "*liv og blod og alt*" ("life, blood, everything"). His sexuality, on the contrary, is proprietorial rather than sacrificial: he lays claim to Nora as "*min dyreste ejendom*" (72); my "most treasured possession" (269), a loveliness that is his alone, totally and utterly.

He mistakes her unwillingness for provocation, and his ardor builds up to a fantasy of first night defloration with other such erotic observances as fit the bridal. Nora's continued refusal precipitates Torvald's assertion of the sexual roles and the marital rights implied in the dolls' house: "What's this? It's just your little game isn't it, my little Nora. Won't! Won't! Am I not your husband . . . ?" (270). His tone of tyrannical playfulness is perfectly captured in the dreadful phrase he finds for her coyness: "*leger spøgefugl*"; playing the "tease-bird" in the coop of their marriage.

Nora is not teasing. Like Dr. Rank, she is fortifying herself with dignity for death, and she learns from the dying man's farewell the virtues of stoicism and acceptance in facing the coming crisis. First Torvald will read Krogstad's letter, then the miracle will happen. His "*liv og blod og alt*" commitment reconfirms the romantic ideal she has imposed on Torvald, and to forestall his magnanimous assumption of blame for her crime, Nora summons up the resolve to perform her ultimate sacrifice.

What follows is momentarily ludicrous:

NORA: (*gropes around her, wild-eyed, seizes Helmer's cloak, wraps it round herself, and whispers quickly, hoarsely, spasmodically.*) Never see him again. Never, never, never. (*Throws her shawl over her head.*) And never see the children again either. Never. Never. Oh, that black icy water. Oh, that bottomless . . . ! If only it were all over! He's got it now. Now he's reading it. Oh no, no! Not yet! Torvald, goodbye . . . and my children. . . . (275)

"This is women's magazine stuff," says John Northam,[4] and he is right to dismiss Nora's final performance as the material for a Harlequin Romance. But Torvald is more accurate in locating the source of her romanticism—not in cheap fiction, but in bad stage melodrama, the late nineteenth-century repository of a faded European tradition. "*Ikke noget komediespil,*" he says (77); "Stop play-acting!" (275). Because life in the dolls' house has been one long *komediespil,* it takes a great effort of the creative imagination to reconsider one's role in a scenario of one's own devising.

Modeling her melodramatic performance, no doubt, on the tragic heroines of the *pièce bien faite* and the *drame à thèse,* Nora has scripted a dénouement that affirms every wish-dream of the boulevard theater, every sentimentally inverted value of the social life. Scribe would have delighted in her performance because it affirms domestic virtue, neatly cuts through the knotty moral problem, and achieves its ends in a splendidly effective theatrical convention. "*En afslutning bør altid være virkningsfuld*" (70), as Torvald's theatrical metaphor puts it; "An exit should always be effective." And Nora, faithful to this Scribean dictum, immerses herself in the sort of French or Danish *komediespil* beloved of theatergoers in Christiania and Bergen. Two plays now occupy the same frame: one is a romantic melodrama in which a noble tragedienne preempts her husband's chivalric assumption of blame and the other is a comic melodrama in which an irate husband abuses his wife as the shiftless imbecile he has always considered her to be. There is an absurd incongruity in the total failure of each to register the other's motivation:

HELMER: (*holds her back.*) Where are you going?

NORA: (*trying to tear herself free.*) You mustn't try to save me, Torvald!

HELMER:	(*reels back.*) True! Is it true what he writes? How dreadful! No, no, it can't possibly be true.
NORA:	It *is* true. I loved you more than anything else in the world.
HELMER:	Don't come to me with a lot of paltry excuses!
NORA:	(*taking a step towards him.*) Torvald . . . !
HELMER:	Miserable woman . . . what is this you have done?
NORA:	Let me go. I won't have you taking the blame for me. You mustn't take it on yourself. (275)

With all the contrary evidence before her, Nora refuses to step out of her Scribean value system and reassess the mise-en-scène of her well-made play. She will rather die than tarnish Torvald's honor. She will rather die than put him to the ultimate test. Torvald's "Stop play-acting!" alerts her to the folly of her performance and the terrible fallibility of her Scribean assumptions. For to redefine her role in the domestic *komediespil*, she must of necessity redefine *his*, and when the comedy abruptly terminates, all she sees before her is a ranting demagogue. This scene is one of those momentary revelations in Ibsen, when in absolute silence the protagonist faces the unspeakable and the unutterable: a sudden falling of the scales of self-deception and a frightening realignment of the contents of her mind. The peripeteia, when it comes, is Sophoclean rather than Scribean. Nora *sees*, with cold clarity, a radically transformed world. Her gaze hardens, focuses unwaveringly upon this man she can no longer recognize as the lover for whom she would sacrifice her life, and she answers his hysteria in calm and chilling monosyllables.

The final scene brings tragic disillusionment to Torvald as well: his fantasy of the ideal doll has been betrayed. The angel entrusted with the task of keeping the house of marriage pure, untarnished, and free of debt turns out to be a fallen woman, a hypocrite, a liar, and a criminal. Like all romantics, his responses are extreme. If his wife is not the pure and perfect "chrysolite," then she must be the "cunning whore" without religion, morality, or sense of duty—her degenerate father's degenerate daughter. "*Liv og blod og alt*" (spilling his life's blood for her) is all forgotten in his bitter condemnation of what she has done to his honor, his reputation, his happiness, his power at the bank, and all, he says, *"for en letsindig kvindes skyld"* (78); "the fault of a feather-brained woman" (276). The language of marital flirtation, with a slight shift in tonality, reveals the brutal contempt beneath the playful condescension. When Nora offers, again, to free him by her death, he dismisses her words as *"fagter"* and *"talemåder"* (78), the grandiloquent "rhetorical gestures" and the "empty platitudes" of bad theater. *His* protestations of domestic affection, *her* impassioned sacrificial sentiments—all has been playacting and pretense. Emptied of significance, their language echoes with the sentimental clichés that they were once incapable of hearing.

Although the scripted playlet of their well-made lives has been thoroughly drained of all conviction, what Torvald next proposes is yet another Scribean scenario, yet another mise-en-scène for the farce that their marriage has become: "The thing must be hushed up at all costs. And as far as you and I are concerned, things must appear to go on exactly as before. But only in the eyes of the world, of course. In other words you'll go on living here; that's understood. But you will not be allowed to bring up the children, I can't trust you with them" (276). The charade is called "preserving appearances," but it is the same charade, with different emphases, that they have always played in the dolls' house. And if Torvald now excludes *"elsk"* and *"lykke"* (79)—"love" and "happiness"—from the new script, the possibility suddenly arises that even these values have been merely the habitual responses of dolls in a puppet play. What he offers her is a ghastly version of what their lives have always been. The only difference is he demands the conscious playing of a text that had once been the unconscious subtext of their marital *komediespil*.

The bits and pieces of Nora's shattered life no sooner fall into a new and realistic pattern than their fortunes are again reversed. When the doorbell rings Torvald in a cold sweat confirms that he possesses the faintheartedness and lack of moral fiber that Krogstad had always suspected. He panics and instructs Nora to hide. She remains motionless and silent. He snatches the letter addressed to his wife, forbids her to see it, and rips it open himself. It is an apology from Krogstad with her incriminating IOU enclosed. "I am saved!" Torvald yelps, "I am saved!" (277). He burns the letters and the bond, confident of erasing the past by destroying the factual evidence, and cheerfully offers to forget the whole unfortunate incident. No harm is done. It has been a Scribean *komediespil* after all with a conventionally happy resolution. So he changes his angle of vision and reads the situation as a piece of pure Sardoodledom in which a devoted wife proves faithful unto death, and the magnanimous husband acknowledges her sacrificial love. Torvald need only revise his mise-en-scène to reflect a more morally conventional dénouement: "Oh, poor little Nora, of course I understand. You can't bring yourself to believe I've forgiven you. But I have, Nora, I swear it. I forgive you everything. I know you did what you did because you loved me" (277).

Nora can no longer participate in his domestic plot. Detached and impassive, she watches him resume the role of birdcatcher to her helpless bird, playing Ken to her Barbie, and proving he is "man enough" to take care of her deficient femininity. But it is *he* who is caught in the cage of socially sanctioned attitudes and grandiloquent phrases. His theater, like Scribe's, has become the inverse expression of the social and emotional life, as discredited a fiction as the women's magazine stuff that might once have shaped Nora's imaginative life: "You loved me as a wife should love her husband. It was simply that you didn't have the experience to judge what was the best way of going about things. But do you think I love you any less for that; just because you don't know how to act on your own responsibility? No, no, you just lean on me, I shall give you all the advice and guidance you need. I wouldn't be a proper man if I didn't find a woman doubly attractive for being so obviously helpless" (278). Here he is again, the "proper man," protector of the "frightened little song-bird," comforter of the "hunted dove" (278). A real man, he assures her, takes immense satisfaction in forgiving his wife from the bottom of his heart: "It's as though it made her his property in a double sense: he has, as it were, given her a new life, and she becomes in a way both his wife and at the same time his child" (278).

"Bird and Birdcatcher": Nora and Torvald

But Nora does not stay to hear these verbal hammer blows on the coffin of their marriage or his offer to subsume her "*vilje og samvittighed*" (81)—her "will and conscience"—to his own discretionary power. The time has come to discard the doll, and she goes into the spare room to take off her "*maskeradedragten*" (80); the "fancy dress" that epitomizes the whole dolls' house masquerade. When she steps back into Torvald's *pièce bien faite* she is dressed for quite another play. Instead of the negligée that he expects for the conventional happy reconciliation of lovebirds, she returns in traveling clothes for a completely unexpected exit.

The uneasy vacillation between Nora's well-made romantic melodrama and Ibsen's parable of spiritual transformation is finally resolved, and Nora's change of clothes becomes the external sign of the doll's extraordinary metamorphosis into the self-reliant and ethically responsible heroine she has always been beneath the Scribean fancy dress. The Nora who finally stops playacting, who discards the masquerade, is a paradigm of the liberated spirits in Ibsen's later plays. She is one of the self-creating women who discover the inner vivifying force that is the God within: authentic existential selfhood, that spark of divine fire that turns inanimate form into living flesh at whatever terrible cost to one's well-being.

The doll dies into womanhood. For only a doll would play the melodramatic suicide beneath the ice and immolate herself for a dream of masculine vainglory. The woman knows better. Nora commits herself to the ensuing tragedy of moral self-education and spiritual self-discovery, the end of Edenic security, and the grievous loss of children, which are the consequences of accepting self-respect and freedom from the dolls' house as the primary conditions of her existence. To make the change, as she has done, is to step out of the nineteenth into the twentieth century and redefine radically the role of the angel in the house, the bird in the pine-twig cage, or the treasured property conditioned to see herself through the eyes of the appropriating male as "*du lille rådvilde, hjælpeløse væsen*" (81); "helpless, perplexed little thing that you are" (278).

A century later, Torvald's language and domestic attitudes may have a ludicrous, anachronistic echo to them, but if they do, the reason is that *A Doll's House* has made it virtually impossible to tolerate the standard Victorian view of the angel without derision. Nora spearheads a cultural revolution in women's sensibility by refusing to accept the traditional view that women hold of themselves, which is absorbed through a process of insidious osmosis from the standard archetypes devised by men. It is not surprising that the locus classicus of nineteenth-century sexual attitudes should feature a female paragon literally shaped and sculpted by a male creator. In W. S. Gilbert's *Pygmalion and Galatea*, written in the same decade as *A Doll's House*, Galatea, a paradigm of self-denying Victorian womanhood, envisions her raison d'être as a perfect man-made artefact:

> A sense that I am made *by* thee *for* thee;
> That I've no will that is not wholly thine:
> That I've no thought, no hope, no enterprise
> That does not own *thee* as its sovereign;
> That I have life, that I may live for thee,
> That I am thine—[5]

Being the ideal woman, the quintessential doll, means being an eternal minister to masculine requirements, a thing without will, autonomy, volition, thought, or ambition distinct from her creator's, being totally dependent, and without other purpose than belonging to her maker.

A RECKONING

Nora is discarding this frame of mind together with her fancy dress and tries to persuade Torvald to see it as the most pernicious fabrication of *les autres*. "Sit down, Torvald," she says to him. "We two have a lot to talk about" (279). For the first time in their eight years of marriage they will now engage in a serious exchange of meaningful views, what Nora calls *"et opgør"* (81), a "reckoning," a domestic settling of moral accounts. Shaw calls it the "discussion," which displaces the conventional dénouement of the Scribean play because it is not so much an unraveling as a complication, a new technical feature (like the incorporation of an unexpected movement into a symphony) that so radically alters dramatic form that we are forced to see the play over again before it becomes fully intelligible. But this is more than a mere debate in which clever intellectual points are scored and more than a domestic argument in which emotional one-upmanship determines the victory. Indeed, Nora never even mentions Torvald's indebtedness to her. Their *"opgør"* is an exorcism of ghostly ideas and beliefs lodged in the soul and clinging to life, and as they speak to each other there is a dramatic revelation of change in which thoughts are reordered and experience reshaped. As in the best plays of Shaw, it is not the protagonists' formulation of carefully reasoned thought that matters in the final confrontation but the process that transforms them from dolls into sentient human beings. And, as Shaw learned from the *"opgør,"* the final conflict is no melodramatic opposition of unequivocal right and wrong but a clarification of unsettled ideals that raises crucial moral questions without closing the issues.

Nora must finally "plumb the depths"—*"komme tilbunds"* (82)—of her own introspective revaluation and then reveal her new-found self as fully as possible in order to be understood. This moral introspection is the force that has driven her through the play in fits and starts of self-recognition, in shafts of dangerous self-revelation that threaten to destroy the comfortable dolls' house life. Now she understands and tries to communicate the altered state of her marriage by making careful distinctions between authentic and inauthentic qualities of being, between "love" and the ephemeral pleasures of merely being "in love," between *"lykke"* and *"lystighed"* (83); "joy" as an indispensable condition of human relationships and "happiness" as the sporadic pleasure that has replaced joy in their lives.

In reevaluating herself she recognizes the role she has played as a passive generator of this kind of happiness: she has been her father's *"dukkebarn"* (82), his "baby doll," and her husband's *"lykkebarn"* (74), the "good luck charm" that safeguards his pleasure. The cost has been an impoverishment of spirit (she sees herself as a beggar in her husband's house) and a trivialization of her human significance (she sees herself as a circus performer living off her trickery). But even worse than this, the entire house has been nothing but a gigantic nursery in which a doll-wife has passed on the values of the dolls' house to her own doll-children thus perpetuating the cycle. The doll's house is not blighted by the hereditary transmission of disease but by the corruption at the very heart of the culture—the perpetuation of ghosts that imprison intellect and feeling in the mind-forged manacles of a moribund value system.

Nora is indeed unfit to bring up her own children, and Torvald's irate words echo in the reader's memory as she comes to understand the precise nature of her failure: "you will not be allowed to bring up the children, I can't trust you with them . . ." (276). But her unfitness has nothing to do with the determinist nonsense about a criminal mother infecting her children and poisoning her home with "evil germs" (233). Her corrupting influence has been cultural, not genetic. She has taught her doll-children to accept deceit and subterfuge as a normative state, and before she can teach them intellectual independence and freedom of spirit she must first instruct herself in this lonely existential enterprise: "*at opdrage mig selv,*" "*få rede på mig selv og på alting udenfor*" (83); "undertake her own educational upbringing" and "come to terms with herself" and with the moral context in which she lives. "You are not the man to help me there," she tells Torvald. "That's something I must do on my own. That's why I'm leaving you. . . . That's why I can't stay here with you any longer" (281). The bird does not turn to the birdcatcher for lessons in freedom.

The shift of emphasis to Torvald's helplessness, trapped and beating in *his* pine-twig cage of custom and convention, lies in a gradual modulation of his tone from arrogant self-confidence to accusatory bluster to a pathetic acknowledgment of Nora's strange new vision. "You frighten me, Nora," he says at the start of their traumatic reckoning, "I don't understand you" (279). His initial response is to strike at her with the weapons of male outrage against the nonconforming woman: he says she is unreasonable, ungrateful, hysterical, out of her mind to leave him, mad, and blind. Later (more charitably) he suggests that she is sick, feverish, delirious—not rebellious, but "indisposed" and therefore irrational. His immediate response is to concede an element of truth in her exaggerated charges and then to offer to teach her to be a better wife. When all else fails, he asserts his prerogative: he refuses to allow her to go—he *forbids* her. But the only power he has ever exercised in the dolls' house is the power she has conceded to him, and there are no longer any grounds on which he can restrain her. She is taking nothing with her, and she has absolved him of all rights to support.

What can he do, now, except invoke the system to which *he* has conceded such extraordinary power? Bar by bar, he defines the social cage in which he is trapped—a construct of duties and obligations, of precedent, authority, social sanctions, religious scruples, and the welter of restrictions that manacle the unfree spirit. His inability to grasp a new truth looks forward to a similar confrontation in Ibsen's *Ghosts*, wherein the convention-bound Pastor Manders upbraids the self-styled freethinker, Mrs. Alving, for flouting the absolute authority of the commandment to honor thy father:

> MANDERS: Have you forgotten that a child is supposed to love and honour its father and mother?
>
> MRS. ALVING: Let's not generalize. The question is: is Oswald supposed to love and honour Captain Alving?
>
> MANDERS: Don't you feel your mother's heart prompting you not to shatter your son's ideals?
>
> MRS. ALVING: But what about the truth?
>
> MANDERS: What about his ideals?
>
> MRS. ALVING: Oh, ideals, ideals! (*Ghosts*, 382)

Ideals and truths, in Ibsen's world, are no longer synonymous, and unless the general and abstract can be validated by living experience, they have no claim on our allegiance. For Torvald, as for the pastor, the claim of the ideal precedes the living proof of its authority. But for Nora, as for Mrs. Alving, the truth that is experienced takes precedence over the ideals of social systems and moral codes that have lost all contact with reality. The conflict, in its most basic form, then, exists between a constellation of abstract and general ideals and a series of particular and specific truths that have been experienced and so challenge received opinion. For the self-liberating heroine, existence is no longer definable as paradigms or roles or duties that smother individuality and obliterate the self. Truth must be felt in the heart, tested on the pulse. "Don't you care what people will say?" asks Torvald, but for Nora the necessity of independent decision displaces conventional conduct. "Isn't your most sacred duty to your husband and children?" he asks, but unless the world of vital relationships can co-exist with self-regard, "duty" merely degenerates into a subjugation of selfhood to forms of codified role-playing. "Haven't you an infallible guide in your religion?" he asks, but when faith congeals into a sanctified system of absolute and inflexible rules, it must be tested against a personal perception of right and wrong. "Don't you have some moral sense?" he asks, but when, as with Antigone, the woman's moral sensibility is based on love and not on law, and when ethics are legislated without concern for humane exceptions to rules, then society no longer satisfies the need of the individual and horrible confusion follows. To the best of her ability, Nora impresses upon Torvald, not an absolute certainty in the rightness of her resolve, but an urgent need to think things out for herself, to clarify, to inquire, to make sense of a world suddenly bereft of infallible guides and unequivocal rules of moral conduct.

The "*opgør*" modulates from its vision of the disoriented individual in society to the specific unhappiness of the Helmer marriage and the breakdown of their relationship. "You don't love me any more" (283) is the rueful conclusion Torvald finally reaches, and Nora has to ease him through the pain into an understanding of their failure and the fallibility of high romantic notions of ideal marriage. She speaks, initially, of the awful gap between her unrealistic expectations and his pathetic performance, of her transference of religious faith into human relationships, and the godlike demands she has made on a mortal husband. She has dreamt of the miraculous, of redemption through the agency of a Savior who will defy the world and take her sins upon himself, who will come forward and say, "Tell the whole world if you like. . . . I am the guilty one" (284).

In the absence of all other solutions to her eight years of patient waiting for significance, Nora has devised her own remedy for the death of spirit in the dolls' house: she has transformed the man into a sacred ideal who will finally give value to her life. Ernest Becker has called this the "romantic solution," a form of self-glorification achieved by attributing to the lover a form of divine perfection to whom one's destiny is inextricably bound. But Nora's romantic solution to the death of absolute value is as fallible as Torvald's social solution to the human dilemma. For no human being, as Becker puts it, can be a godlike everything to another, and no human relationship can bear the burden of godhood or reflect an ideal image of ourselves: "No human partner can offer this assurance because the partner is real. However much we may idealize and idolize him, he inevitably reflects earthly decay and imperfection. And as he is our ideal measure of value, this imperfection falls back upon us."[6] It is Torvald, in the final analysis, who has been Nora's angel in the house, the redeemer whose miraculous assumption of her sin would, she believes, reciprocate the miracle of *her* sacrifice, and Nora's refusal during their eight-year marriage to acknowledge his manifest human imperfection has turned him into the doll-as-God.

For Nora to have lived in hope and dread of the miraculous has been a romantic folly, a failure to distinguish between human realities and spiritual ideals. But now Nora's priorities are clear. In Torvald's world, the abstract ideal (however emptied of value) still takes precedence over the ethical, the real. No man, he tells Nora, will sacrifice his *honor* for *the one he loves*. But for Nora, there can be no suspension of human feeling in the name of some abstraction. Hundreds and thousands of women, she indicates, have put the claims of love above the vague and egocentric claims of honor. And this becomes another major difference between her existential value system and his, another fundamental difference between the Antigones and the Creons of the world. Nora must leave her husband, not because he has failed her as God, but because he has failed her as a man—as a caring husband, as a lover, as a decent and compassionate human being. When romantic impossibility fails to materialize as "miracle," the most wonderful thing one can hope for in the circumstances is a form of moral support, an acknowledgment from the other that we all live in the shadow of human imperfection. Torvald's betrayal of her most basic expectations of a husband's love is Nora's most profound disappointment. Insofar as the image of the doll-god has been a figment of her romantic need for significance in the dolls' house, her acceptance of its loss is an index of her existential growth. But what remains when this God is dead is *less,* she implies, than the kind of husband she needs to sustain her everyday existence:

> But you neither think nor talk like the man I would want to share my life with. When you had got over your fright—and you weren't concerned about me but only about what might happen to you— and when all danger was past, you acted as though nothing had happened. I was your little sky-lark again, your little doll, exactly as before; except you would have to protect it twice as carefully as before, now that it had shown itself to be so weak and fragile. Torvald, that was the moment I realised that for eight years I'd been living with a stranger, and had borne him three children. (285)

She rejects Torvald not because he has offended a teleological ideal but because he is incapable of moral sympathy, compassion for her suffering, or imagination. She looks at him, and can recognize neither a god nor a husband in the strange and empty form she sees. Now Torvald *feels* the truth of what she says, and his immediate sensation is that of a sudden abyss opening up between them—a familiar image in Ibsen of the chasm separating the reality of the fallen world from the illusions of Eden. For the first time in the "*opgør,*" Torvald acquires the self-consciousness of the birdcatcher who suddenly sees himself as the bird, and he feels a quake of fear at the infinite distance between him and his wife. "Is there no way we might bridge it," he asks, acknowledging with a strange new courage his own capacity to change, "*at blive en anden*" (87); "to become another kind of man."

Nora, who has been an accomplice in the kind of man he *has been,* acknowledges the possibility of a metamorphosis that she, as doll-wife, is powerless to inspire—except by leaving him, by removing his doll and the temptation to lapse into habitual modes of thought and conduct.

She ends her long confrontation by ritualizing her departure, by robing herself in the clothes of a traveler and the black shawl of the tarantella. And then she performs a strange ad hoc ceremony of divorce, beyond all legal formality, that confers upon them both a new-found freedom from the duties and obligations and bondage of the dolls' house: *"Der må være fuld frihed på begge side"* (88); "There must be full freedom on both sides," she says, liberating him as she liberates herself from their destructive relationship. She returns his ring and the household keys, and Torvald, compelled despite his distress into participation, ritually returns the ring she gave to him in marriage. She discreates the wife, the mother, the housekeeper by bereaving herself of all the roles and connections that had both sustained and destroyed her as an independent human being, estranging herself from her stranger husband, and finally committing herself to the terrible uncertainty of her venture, for good or ill, into an undiscovered country: "I've no idea," she freely admits, "what I might turn out to be" (285).

Like all such leaps of faith, Nora's is a leap in the dark, an act of heroic courage that leaves her dispossessed, defenseless, and undefined. But it also frees her to become the woman she might turn out to be, the essential self that the newfound freedom of her existence must now define. Catastrophe and loss are inextricably linked, in Ibsen's dénouements, with exhilaration and hope—the death of the doll with the awakening of the woman, the fear and trembling of the unknown with the distant vision of marriage transformed, a world of strangers with a democracy of kindred souls. "Nora, can I never be anything more to you than a stranger?" he asks (286), and she, no longer believing in miracles, nevertheless concedes to the possibility of *"forvandl[ing]"* (88)—of "change," "transformation," "metamorphosis"—as the saving force in their lives. The "miraculous" dissociated from romantic fantasy and God's prerogative is finally restored as the human capacity for self-renewal and cultural reintegration.

> HELMER: Name it, this miracle of miracles!
>
> NORA: Both you and I would have to change to the point where . . .
> Oh, Torvald, I don't believe in miracles any more.
>
> HELMER: But I *will* believe. Name it! Change to the point where . . . ?
>
> NORA: Where we could make a real marriage of our lives together,
> Goodbye!
> (*She goes out through the hall door.*) (286)

The last beat of the play is Torvald's. The birdcatcher, caught, confounded, and panic-stricken in the emptiness of his life, in a momentary epiphany of hope, suddenly glimpses "freedom's gateway" in Nora's vision of "*det vidunderligste*" (88), which places "the most wonderful of all things" at the disposal of the most ordinary of men and challenges him to believe in her spiritual revolution:

> HELMER: (*sinks down on a chair near the door, and covers his face with his hands.*) Nora! Nora! (*He rises and looks round.*) Empty! She's gone! (*With sudden hope.*) The miracle of miracles . . . ?
> (*The heavy sound of a door being slammed is heard from below.*) (286)

Maybe they will both break their wings in the bid for freedom. Maybe they will find a way to fly. The play leaves the issues open for the modern world as Nora slams the door on an outmoded nineteenth-century world of moribund values, sexual perversity, dead ideas, petrified faith, false gods, empty romanticism, self-deprecation, determinist theology, small-minded moralism, and the thousand other ills that the dolls' house mentality is heir to.

conclusion

After the doll's house, what then? A minor grubstreet enterprise, ever since Nora's door-slamming exit, has been the revision of Ibsen's dénouement and the concoction of a dire and prophetic afterlife for his heroine. In 1890, Walter Besant published a sequel bristling with moral outrage against misguided Norwegian heresy, which Shaw rebutted in "Still after the Doll's House." Eleanor Marx and Israel Zangwill enlarged upon Besant's work in their parodic inversion of socialist idealism in which a contrite Nora submits to Torvald's plans for keeping up bourgeois appearances and accepts her banishment from the nursery and the marital bed. It was Eleanor Marx's satyr play that, during the course of her domestic life with her common-law husband, decisively replaced Ibsen's original in her wretched experience of a liberated woman's hopes eternally deferred.[1]

Nora's decision to strike out into a brave new world finds its only meaningful sequel in the history of Victorian woman's difficult journey from 1879 to 1990, in her struggle against the dragons in the path that impress her biological limitations upon her, that persuade her to believe that anatomy is destiny, and that legislate her out of political influence and economic self-sufficiency. There is no doubt that much has changed in the modern world to mitigate the anguish of Nora's choice in 1879. In one of the last sequels to Ibsen's play, written by Clare Booth Luce in 1970,[2] another Nora—liberated by the pill from inevitable motherhood, liberated intellectually by her education, and liberated from culturally conditioned self-deprecation by feminist writers from de Beauvoir to Mary Ellman and Kate Millett—closes the door, very gently, on a much-loved husband for whom the "miracle" has not yet happened. This Nora will find a job in computer programming, helped by other women who have discovered a new cultural identity in the late twentieth century.

If Ibsen's brightening vision failed the Victorian woman (as Eleanor Marx put it) and if Nora's dream of the miraculous is tragically qualified in Mrs. Alving (*Ghosts*), Hedda Gabler (*Hedda Gabler*), and Rebekka West (*Rosmersholm*), then the contemporary Nora may with some confidence look back to a time when the price of slamming the door was a kind of death. But the contemporary Nora will also know that old attitudes die hard and that computer programming is no absolute defense against resurgent chauvinism or blank despair of the miraculous. The 1970s was a great celebratory decade for Nora. The play, as it were, was rediscovered in the spirit of women's liberation with two motion pictures released in the same year, with Claire Bloom and Jane Fonda playing Ibsen's Nora. But there was a third film made for German video in 1973 by Rainer Werner Fassbinder and called *Nora Helmer*, the title unmistakably insisting on the husband's wife and the director resolutely denying the possibility of a miracle in the modern world. Fassbinder's Nora stays home, not because there are children to bind her but because there is nowhere for her to go and because most people learn to accommodate themselves (as Judge Brack tells Hedda) to the inevitable. There could be no more depressing sequel to Ibsen's play, no more despairing rejoinder to his vision of humankind's capacity for self-transformation.[3]

Debate and controversy continue to whirl around *A Doll's House*. Is Ibsen our contemporary? Or can we now safely relegate *A Doll's House* to the museum of outmoded plays? Is his vision of creative change still viable? Or does Nora remain a romantic even in her final choice? Disagreement is most vociferous, as one might expect, in the world of Ibsen scholarship, where Hermann Weigand's once powerful voice condemned Nora as a self-dramatizing and petulant naïf who undergoes no metamorphosis and whose departure is merely perverse. Endorsed by psychoanalysts who diagnose Nora as a pathological liar and hysteric, emotionally repressed, and power hungry, this view of

Nora is fairly familiar in dramatic criticism from 1902 to the late 1980s.[4] To the best of my knowledge, no actress has yet gone the entire hysterical route. But each time Nora is embodied in performance, there is a new reading and a new interpretation of both character and play. Is the real Nora Claire Bloom's all-knowing, calculating woman whose decision to strike out for independence is made long before the curtain rises? Or is she Liv Ullmann's confused woman, partly abhorring her doll's existence and partly enjoying it in moments of unquestioning pleasure?[5]

What I offer in this reading of *A Doll's House* as a "myth of transformation" is a blueprint for performance in the theater of my own imagination. I have based my interpretation on certain assumptions that I hope my readers will share and that, in conclusion, I would like to restate:

1) The play, despite versions by Frances Lord, Ingmar Bergman, and Rainer Fassbinder, is *not* called *Nora* or *Nora Helmer*. It is not, in other words, a monodrama about individual consciousness but a play in which many different choices are held in delicate equilibrium, in which the *tvertimod*—the contradictions in human experience—structure form and challenge our response. Nora exists in a nexus of relationships with other people in the great dolls' house of the social world, and the play asks us to see how its characters live in that world, how each devises strategies of painful change, creative accommodation, or apathetic resignation to the inevitable.

2) The key to my reading of Ibsen's text is the lifeline Mrs. Linde throws to the wrecked and desperate Krogstad: the great consoling hope that it is possible "to become another sort of human being"; "*at . . . blevet en anden*" (67). The salvation of humankind is the individual's capacity for change, for transformation, either in vitally creative relationship with another or by a difficult reordering of the contents of the intellectual and moral life. This capacity is not Nora's sole prerogative. Krogstad is utterly transformed just as, in the last few moments of the play, the light begins to break in on Torvald. I have spoken of this optimistic vision as a form of secular faith graced with a terminology that suggests an older tradition of faith in which

"miracle" connotes the impossible made possible by divine interven-tion. In *A Doll's House* we are all, by implication, blessed with the capacity for miracle as possibility, and this form of secular faith is what I understand by existentialism.

3) The governing idea of the play, as I read it, is "transformation," not only as an existential concept, but as a principle of dramatic com-position that supports Ibsen's vision in every theatrical detail: the lan-guage is transformed from the empty colloquialism of "marvellous" through the pseudoreligious rhetoric of the marvellous as "miracle" to the incorporation of the miraculous into the world of ordinary human endeavor; the stage set is transformed, both physically and in the mind of the protagonist, from a secure domestic Eden to a prison world of devastated value; the genres tragedy, melodrama, and the well-made play are transformed into an innovative modern form significantly dif-ferent from its constitutive elements; the doll is transformed into a sentient and self-conscious human being through the ancient ritual of dance; and the fated naturalist universe is transformed into a world of creative and dynamic change by the protagonist's commitment to difficult choice and painful life decisions.

notes and references

1. The Spiritual Revolution

1. Brian Downs, *Ibsen: The Intellectual Background* (Cambridge: Cambridge University Press, 1946), 6.

2. See especially Brian Johnston, *Text and Supertext in Ibsen's Drama* (University Park: Pennsylvania State University Press), for a detailed Hegelian reading of *A Doll's House* and other Ibsen plays.

3. Michael Meyer, *Ibsen: A Biography* (New York: Doubleday, 1971), 807–8.

4. "Et Vers," in "Digte," *Henrik Ibsen: Samlede Værker*, vol. 4 (Kristiania: Gyldendalske Boghandel, 1914), 309. For a translation of this poem see John Northam, "A Verse," *Ibsen's Poems* (Oslo: Norwegian University Press, 1986), 135.

5. Quoted in Frederick and Lise-Lone Marker, "The First Nora," *Contemporary Approaches to Ibsen*, vol. 2, ed. Daniel Haakonsen (Oslo: Universitetsforlaget, 1971), 89.

2. The Importance of the Work

1. George Steiner, *The Death of Tragedy* (London: Faber & Faber, 1961), 292.

2. Kate Millett, *Sexual Politics* (Garden City, N.Y.: Doubleday, 1970), 115.

3. Johnston, "*A Doll House*, or 'The Fortunate Fall,'" in *Text and Supertext*, 137–64.

4. Carol Strongin Tufts, "Recasting *A Doll House*: Narcissism as Character Motivation in Ibsen's Play," *Comparative Drama* 20 (Summer 1986): 140–59.

5. Frank Wedekind, quoted by Rolf Fjelde, "Peer Gynt, Naturalism, and the Dissolving Self," *Drama Review* 13 (Winter 1968): 29.

3. Critical Reception

1. Frances Lord, *Nora; or, A Doll's House* (London: Griffith Farran, 1890), xiv.

2. Quoted in "*A Doll's House*: Commentary," *The Oxford Ibsen*, vol. 5, 457; hereafter cited in the text.

3. M. W. Brun, quoted in Frederick and Lise-Lone Marker, "The First Nora: Notes on the World Premiere of *A Doll's House*," *Contemporary Approaches to Ibsen*, ed. Daniel Haakonsen (Oslo: Universitetsforlaget, 1970), 86.

4. See Frederick and Lise-Lone Marker, "The First Nora," 87.

5. Erik Bøgh, quoted in Frederick and Lise-Lone Marker, "The First Nora," 89.

6. Eleanor Marx, quoted in Yvonne Kapp, *Eleanor Marx*, vol. 2, *The Crowded Years* (London: Lawrence and Wishart, 1976), 103.

7. Eleanor Marx, quoted in Ronald Florence, *Marx's Daughters* (New York: Dial Press, 1975), 588.

8. Ian Britain, "A Transplanted Doll's House: Ibsenism, Feminism and Socialism in Late-Victorian and Edwardian England," *Transformations in Modern European Drama*, ed. Ian Donaldson (Atlantic Highlands, N.J.: Humanities Press, 1983), 14–54.

9. Bernard Shaw, "Fragments of a Fabian Lecture, 1890," in *Shaw and Ibsen: Bernard Shaw's The Quintessence of Ibsenism and Related Writings*, ed. with an introductory essay by J. L. Wisenthal (Toronto: University of Toronto Press, 1979), 89.

10. Harley Granville-Barker, quoted in "*A Doll's House*: Commentary," *The Oxford Ibsen*, vol. 5, 460.

11. William Archer, quoted in "*A Doll's House*: Commentary," *The Oxford Ibsen*, vol. 5, 460.

12. Bernard Shaw, "A Play by Henrik Ibsen in London," in *Shaw and Ibsen*, ed. Wisenthal, 76–77.

13. William Archer, "The Mausoleum of Ibsen," *Fortnightly Review* 54, n.s. (1893): 77–91, reprinted in *Henrik Ibsen: A Critical Anthology*, ed. James McFarlane (Harmondsworth: Penguin Books, 1970), 151–55; Bernard Shaw, "Is Mr Buchanan a Critic with a Wooden Head?" *Pall Mall Gazette* 13 June 1889, reprinted in *Shaw and Ibsen*, ed. Wisenthal, 78–80.

14. William Archer, extracts from "The Mausoleum of Ibsen," quoted in *Critical Anthology*, ed. McFarlane, 152.

15. Sean O'Casey, *Juno and the Paycock* (1924), in *Three Plays* (London: Macmillan, 1969), 20–21.

16. Joseph P. Dannenburg, "Playing Ibsen in the Badlands," *Theatre* 6 (August 1906), in *Ibsen: The Critical Heritage*, ed. Michael Egan (London: Routledge & Kegan Paul, 1972), 459.

17. Edwin E. Slosson, "Ibsen as an Interpreter of American Life," *Independent*, 31 May 1906, in *Ibsen: The Critical Heritage*, 452; hereafter cited in the text.

18. Robert A. Schanke, *Ibsen in America: A Century of Change* (Metuchen, N.J.: Scarecrow Press, 1988), 38; hereafter cited in the text.

19. Edward Dithmar, quoted in *Ibsen in America*, 15–16.

20. William Dean Howells, quoted in *Ibsen: The Critical Heritage*, 446.

4. Translating *Et Dukkehjem* into *A Doll's House*

1. Charles Dickens, *Our Mutual Friend* (London: Hazell, Watson & Viney, n.d.), 581. This edition is printed from the one carefully corrected by the author in 1867–68.

2. Many North American critics and scholars prefer to use Rolf Fjelde's title, *A Doll House*.

3. Alfred, Lord Tennyson, "Vastness," quoted in Walter E. Houghton, *The Victorian Frame of Mind, 1830–1870* (New Haven, Conn.: Yale University Press, 1957), 341.

4. *Ibsen: A Doll's House and Other Plays*, trans. Peter Watts (Harmondsworth: Penguin Books, 1965), 333.

5. Arthur Miller, *Death of a Salesman* (New York: Viking Press, 1964), 65.

6. Lord, *Nora*, 62.

7. *The Collected Works of Henrik Ibsen*, vol. 7, trans. William Archer (London: William Heinemann, 1906), 76n.

5. Visual Metaphors and Performance

1. Virginia Woolf, *The Death of the Moth* (London: Hogarth Press, 1942), 108.

2. I refer here to Chris Barreca's design for the American Ibsen Theatre (1984), Meyerhold's "constructivist" set for his Moscow production in 1922, and Robert Gardiner's paper cutout set in the 1987 production for the Frederic Wood Theatre in Vancouver.

3. John Northam, "Ibsen's Search for the Hero," in *Ibsen: A Collection of Critical Essays*, ed. Rolf Fjelde (Englewood Cliffs, N.J.: Prentice-Hall, 1965), 105.

4. Inga-Stina Ewbank, "Ibsen and the Language of Women," in *Women Writing and Writing about Women*, ed. Mary Jacobus (London: Croom Helm, 1979), 128.

6. Tragedy without Tears: Form and Genre

1. James McFarlane, Introduction, *The Oxford Ibsen*, vol. 5, 2.

2. Bernard Shaw, "The Technical Novelty in Ibsen's Plays" (1913), in *Shaw and Ibsen*, ed. J. L. Wisenthal, 218; hereafter cited in the text.

3. W. B. Yeats, "Meru," *The Collected Poems of W. B. Yeats* (London: Macmillan, 1958), 333.

4. Sophocles, *Oedipus Rex*, trans. Dudley Fitts and Robert Fitzgerald (1949), rpt. in *The Experience of Literature*, ed. Lionel Trilling (New York: Holt, Rinehart & Winston, 1967), 30.

5. Bernard Shaw, Preface, *Mrs Warren's Profession* (1894), in *Plays Unpleasant* (Harmondsworth: Penguin Books, 1957), 185.

6. Stephen S. Stanton, ed., *Camille and Other Plays* (New York: Hill & Wang, 1957).

7. Eugene Scribe, quoted by Stanton, Introduction, *Camille and Other Plays*, vii n. 2.

8. Harley Granville-Barker, "The Coming of Ibsen" (1884), in *Critical Anthology*, ed. McFarlane, 103.

9. Bernard Shaw, "The Technical Novelty in Ibsen's Plays," in *Shaw and Ibsen*, ed. Wisenthal, 212.

10. Compare Stanton, Introduction, *Camille and Other Plays*, xii–xiii.

11. Bernard Shaw, "The Technical Novelty," 210, 213.

12. Bernard Shaw, "Is Mr Buchanan a Critic with a Wooden Head?" (1889), in *Shaw and Ibsen*, ed. Wisenthal, 79.

13. For the theory underlying the realistic drama, see George J. Becker, *Realism in Modern Literature* (New York: Frederick Ungar, 1980).

14. Bernard Shaw, *Heartbreak House* (Harmondsworth: Penguin Books, 1967), 14.

7. Nora's Mirror Images: Anne Marie, Krogstad, Rank

1. Clement Scott, "A Doll's House," *Theatre* (1889), in *Ibsen: The Critical Heritage*, ed. Egan, 114.

8. "The Problem of Women": Nora and Mrs. Linde

1. Quoted in Meyer, *Ibsen: A Biography*, 774–75.

2. Millett, *Sexual Politics*, 152, 156.

3. H. D. F. Kitto, *Form and Meaning in Drama* (London: Methuen, 1960), 270.

4. Inga-Stina Ewbank, "Ibsen and the Language of Women," 118.

5. Erich Fromm, *The Fear of Freedom* (London: Routledge & Kegan Paul, 1942); hereafter cited in the text.

9. "Bird and Birdcatcher": Nora and Torvald

1. *"Fugl og Fuglfænger," "Digte," Henrik Ibsen: Samlede Værker,* 4:169–70; trans. J. Northam, *Ibsen's Poems,* 27.

2. Jean-Paul Sartre, *The Flies and In Camera* (London: Hamish Hamilton, 1948), 166.

3. Evert Sprinchorn, "Ibsen and the Actors," in *Ibsen and the Theatre,* ed. Errol Durbach (London: Macmillan, 1980), 122.

4. John Northam, "Ibsen's Search for the Hero," 106.

5. W. S. Gilbert, *Pygmalion and Galatea,* in *Original Plays by W. S. Gilbert* (London: Chatto & Windus, 1925), 58.

6. Ernest Becker, *The Denial of Death* (New York: The Free Press, 1973), 166.

Conclusion

1. See Ian Britain, "A Transplanted Doll's House," 14–54.

2. Clare Booth Luce, *"A Doll's House, 1970,"* in *Images of Women in Literature,* ed. Mary Anne Ferguson (Boston: Houghton Mifflin, 1973), 358–69.

3. H. Neville Davies, "Not Just a Bang and a Whimper: The Inconclusiveness of Ibsen's *A Doll's House," Critical Quarterly* 24, no. 3 (1982): 38–39, 42.

4. Sprinchorn, "Ibsen and the Actors," 130 n. 5.

5. I am grateful to Joan Templeton for showing me her as yet unpublished paper, "Nora on the American Stage, 1894–1975: Acting the Integral Text," in which she discusses the Bloom and Ullmann performances.

selected bibliography

Primary Works

A Doll's House. In *The Oxford Ibsen.* Vol. 5. Translated and edited by James McFarlane. London: Oxford University Press, 1961.

Digte (Poems). In *Henrik Ibsen: Samlede Værker.* Vol. 4. Kristiania og København: Gyldendalske Boghandel, 1914.

Et Dukkehjem. In *Henrik Ibsen: Samlede Værker.* Vol. 6. Kristiania og København: Gyldendalske Boghandel, 1914.

Ghosts. In *The Oxford Ibsen.* Vol. 5. Translated and edited by James McFarlane. London: Oxford University Press, 1961.

Hedda Gabler. In *The Oxford Ibsen.* Vol. 7. Translated by Jens Arup; edited by James McFarlane. London: Oxford University Press, 1966.

Ibsen's Poems. Translated by John Northam. Oslo: Norwegian University Press, 1986.

John Gabriel Borkman. In *The Oxford Ibsen.* Vol. 8. Translated by James McFarlane. London: Oxford University Press, 1977.

Peer Gynt. In *The Oxford Ibsen.* Vol. 3. Translated by Christopher Fry; edited by James McFarlane. London: Oxford University Press, 1972.

Secondary Works

Books and Parts of Books

Britain, Ian. "A Transplanted Doll's House: Ibsenism, Feminism and Socialism in Late-Victorian and Edwardian England." In *Transformations in Modern Drama,* edited by Ian Donaldson, 14–54. Atlantic Highlands, N.J.: Humanities Press, 1983. A history of Ibsen's reception in England, and the political and literary climate prevailing in the Victorian and Edwardian period.

Deer, Irving. "Ibsen's Self-Reflexivity in *A Doll's House* and *The Masterbuilder.*" In *Within the Dramatic Spectrum,* edited by Karelisa V. Hartigan, 35–44. Lanhan: University Press of America, 1986. Playacting and metatheater in Ibsen's plays.

Downs, Brian W. *Ibsen: The Intellectual Background.* Cambridge, England: Cambridge University Press, 1946. Ibsen's place in the ethical, religious, and historical thought of his time.

Durbach, Errol. "Ibsen's Liberated Heroines and the Fear of Freedom." In *Contemporary Approaches to Ibsen,* vol. 5, edited by Daniel Haakonsen, 11–23. Oslo: Universitetsforlaget, 1985. Nora's place in Ibsen's evolving concept of freedom.

Egan, Michael, ed. *Ibsen: The Critical Heritage.* London: Routledge & Kegan Paul, 1972. Reviews, articles, and criticism by Ibsen's contemporaries.

Ewbank, Inga-Stina. "Ibsen and the Language of Women." In *Women Writing and Writing about Women,* edited by Mary Jacobus, 114–32. London: Croom Helm, 1979. A sociolinguistic study of how "man enforces on woman a type of behaviour *and* a language to go with it."

Hornby, Richard. "The Ethical Leap: *A Doll House.*" In *Patterns in Ibsen's Middle Plays.* Lewisburg, Penn.: Bucknell University Press, 1981, 89–119. The nature of the "leap" from Kierkegaard's aesthetic level of life to the ethical level in Nora's development.

Johnston, Brian. "*A Doll House* or 'The Fortunate Fall.'" In *Text and Supertext in Ibsen's Drama.* University Park: Pennsylvania State University Press, 1989, 137–64. The play in the context of Ibsen's evolving Hegelian idea structures.

Marker, Frederick and Lise-Lone. "The First Nora: Notes on the World Premiere of *A Doll's House.*" In *Contemporary Approaches to Ibsen,* vol. 2, edited by Daniel Haakonsen, 84–100. Oslo: Universitetsforlaget, 1971. A performance history and critical responses to *A Doll's House* in 1879.

Meyer, Michael. *Ibsen: A Biography.* New York: Doubleday, 1971. A single-volume edition, this is the most comprehensive biography of Ibsen to date.

Northam, John. "*A Doll's House.*" In *Ibsen's Dramatic Method: A Study of the Prose Dramas.* London: Faber & Faber, 1953. A pioneering study of Ibsen's stagecraft.

——— "Ibsen's Search for the Hero." In *Ibsen: A Collection of Critical Essays,* edited by Rolf Fjelde, 91–108. Englewood Cliffs, N.J.: Prentice-Hall, 1965. An analytical study of Nora's development into a tragic heroine.

Quigley, Austin E. "Ibsen: *A Doll's House.*" In *The Modern Stage and Other Worlds,* 91–114. New York: Methuen, 1985. A complex study of the ambivalent value systems in the play and Ibsen's subtle avoidance of solutions.

Saari, Sandra. "Female Become Human: Nora Transformed." In *Contemporary Approaches to Ibsen,* vol. 6, edited by Bjørn Hemmer and Vigdis Ystad, 41–55. Oslo: Norwegian University Press, 1988. Changes to the draft material reveal Ibsen's belief that men and women show no essential difference in their spiritual makeup.

Shafer, Yvonne, ed. *Approaches to Teaching Ibsen's A Doll House.* New York: Modern Language Association of America, 1985. An eclectic collection of essays emphasizing the diversity of critical approaches to the play. -

Shaw, Bernard. "'The Quintessence of Ibsenism' and Related Writings." In *Shaw and Ibsen,* edited with an introductory essay by J. L. Wisenthal. Toronto: University of Toronto Press, 1979. A complete collection of Shaw's comments on *A Doll's House.*

Sprinchorn, Evert. "Ibsen and the Actors." In *Ibsen and the Theatre,* edited by Errol Durbach, 118–30. London: Macmillan, 1980. The play has degenerated into a star vehicle, and we have lost sight of the reverse side of the noble feminist.

Stanton, Stephen S., ed. Introduction to *Camille and Other Plays.* New York: Hill & Wang, 1957. An anthology of the type of well-made drama that Ibsen subverts, with a good introduction on form and genre.

Weigand, Hermann J. "*A Doll's House.*" In *The Modern Ibsen: A Reconsideration.* New York: Henry Holt & Co., 1925. An influential interpretation of Nora as a playacting hysteric who undergoes no significant spiritual or intellectual change.

Journal Articles

Baruch, Elaine Hoffman. "Ibsen's *Doll House*: A Myth for Our Time." *Yale Review* 69 3 (1980):374–87. Feminist reading of Nora as mythic hero, "a rehabilitated Eve who has the courage to leave the garden in search of knowledge" (374).

Davies, H. Neville. "Not Just a Bang and a Whimper: The Inconclusiveness of Ibsen's *A Doll's House.*" *Critical Quarterly* 24 3 (1982):33–43. "Ibsen's main plot is unresolvably inconclusive. It ends with a question mark" (42).

Dietrich, R. F. "Nora's Change of Dress: Weigand Revisited." *The Theatre Annual* 36 (1981):20–40. "Nora is not really fighting for equality; rather she is scheming for supremacy" (38).

Ganz, Arthur. "Miracle and Vine Leaves: An Ibsen Play Rewrought." *PMLA* 94 1 (1979): 9–21. Imagistic and structural affinities between *A Doll's*

House and *Hedda Gabler*—"both works are finally about a transcendent quest for the self" (11).

Rosenberg, Marvin. "Ibsen vs. Ibsen or: Two Version of *A Doll's House.*" *Modern Drama* 12 2 (1969):187–96. A comparison of Ibsen's drafts, in which Nora is first ennobled and then shown as a fallible woman developing moral intelligence.

Tufts, Carol Strongin. "Recasting *A Doll House*: Narcissism as Character Motivation in Ibsen's Play." *Comparative Drama* 20 2 (1986):140–59. A negation of the romantic celebration of the supremacy of the individual: Nora exemplifies an unappealing narcissism as the key factor in all her motives.

Templeton, Joan. "The *Doll House* Backlash: Criticism, Feminism, and Ibsen." *PMLA* 104 1 (1989):28–40. A counterblast to the school of criticism that reads Nora as a selfish and cunning minx.

Van Laan, Thomas F. "The Ending of *A Doll House* and Augier's *Maître Guérin.*" *Comparative Drama* 17 4 (1983–84):297–317. A comparative study of two well-made plays in which the wife leaves her husband, and "the action moves inward from external incidents to mental and psychological phenomena." (314).

index

the author

Errol Durbach is professor and head of the Theatre Department at the University of British Columbia, in Vancouver, where he teaches courses in theater history, modern drama, and comparative drama. He holds degrees from Rhodes University in South Africa, Cambridge, and London where he was awarded a Ph.D. for a study of the *Kindermord* motif in drama. His publications include many articles on modern and comparative drama, from Euripides and Shakespeare to Pinter and Athol Fugard. In 1978 he edited the papers delivered at the Ibsen Sesquicentennial conference held at the University of British Columbia and published as *Ibsen and the Theatre*. His best known work on Ibsen is *"Ibsen the Romantic": Analogues of Paradise in the Later Plays* (1982). At present, he is working on a study of erotic tragedy.